Winning in 2012

CQ Press's Guide to the Elections

Bob Benenson

Los Angeles | London | New Delhi
Singapore | Washington DC

Los Angeles | London | New Delhi
Singapore | Washington DC

FOR INFORMATION:

CQ Press

An Imprint of SAGE Publications, Inc.

2455 Teller Road

Thousand Oaks, California 91320

E-mail: order@sagepub.com

SAGE Publications Ltd.

1 Oliver's Yard

55 City Road

London EC1Y 1SP

United Kingdom

SAGE Publications India Pvt. Ltd.

B 1/I 1 Mohan Cooperative Industrial Area

Mathura Road, New Delhi 110 044

India

SAGE Publications Asia-Pacific Pte. Ltd.

3 Church Street

#10-04 Samsung Hub

Singapore 049483

Image credits: Photo, page 1: AP Photo/The White House, Pete
Souza. Photo, page 8: Chip Somodevilla/Getty Images. photo,
page 12: AP Photo/Charles Dharapak. Photo, page 15: Bryan
Smith/ZUMA Press/Corbis. Photo, page 18: Chip
Somodevilla/Getty Images. Photo, page 19: David L Ryan/The
Boston Globe via Getty Images. Photo, page 21: AP Photo/
Paul Sancya, File. Photo, page 22: DON EMMERT/AFP/Getty
Images. Photo, page 27: Alex Wong/Getty Images. Photo, page
31: AP Photo/Rick Bowmer, File. Photo, page 34: AP Photo/
Charles Dharapak. Photo, page 36: Photo by Afghan
Presidential Palace via Getty Images. Photo, page 45: Julie
Denesha For The Washington Post via Getty Images. Photo,
page 47: Benjamin J. Myers/Corbis. Photo, page 48: AP Photo/
AJ Mast. Photo, page 50: Photo by Jonathan Wiggs/The
Boston Globe via Getty Images. Cartoon, page 10: © Tribune
Media Services, Inc. All Rights Reserved. Reprinted with
permission. Cartoon, page 25: TOLES © 2012 The
Washington Post. Reprinted with permission of UNIVERSAL
UCLICK. All rights reserved. Cartoon, page 26: By RJ Matson,
Roll Call, politicalcartoons.com.

Printed in the United States of America

Library of Congress Cataloging-in-Publication Data

A catalog record of this book is available from the Library of
Congress.

ISBN 978-1-4522-2788-7

This book is printed on acid-free paper.

Acquisitions Editor: Charisse Kiino

Editorial Assistant: Nancy Loh

Production Editor: Laureen Gleason

Copy Editor: QuADS Prepress (P) Ltd.

Typesetter: C&M Digitals (P) Ltd.

Proofreader: Gretchen Treadwell

Cover Designer: Paula Goldstein, Blue Bungalow Design

Marketing Manager: Jonathan Mason

Permissions Editor: Adele Hutchinson

Certified Chain of Custody
Promoting Sustainable Forestry
www.sfiprogram.org
SFI-01268

SFI label applies to text stock

12 13 14 15 16 10 9 8 7 6 5 4 3 2 1

Contents

About the Author

Bob Benenson is a veteran political analyst who wrote and edited at *Congressional Quarterly* in Washington, D.C., for thirty years. For eleven years (1998–2009), he was *CQ*'s politics editor and, over six election cycles, headed the company's well-regarded team that covered presidential, congressional, and gubernatorial elections, the longest tenure for anyone who held that position. Bob—a 1977 graduate of Michigan State University—relocated to Chicago in summer 2011 with his wife Barb, an Illinois native, and is currently a freelance journalist and blogger.

President Obama on May 1, 2011, watches an update on the U.S. military raid in Pakistan in which the terrorist leader Osama bin Laden—a fugitive for almost ten years after the 9/11 attacks he orchestrated—was killed. Also in attendance were Vice President Joseph R. Biden (*in front of Obama*), Defense Secretary Robert Gates (*lower right*), and Secretary of State Hillary Rodham Clinton (*behind Gates*).

Obama: Timely Rebound, but Reelection Not Assured

Few political commentators in the spring of 2012 were willing to deem President Barack Obama as the odds-on favorite to win a second term in the November elections. His job approval percentages in polls had improved from their nadir of around 40 percent at the midpoint of his four-year term (Figure 1). But they still teetered just around the crucial 50 percent mark, as the nation continued to make only a modest recovery from a deep economic recession.

Yet most observers viewed the Democratic incumbent as having at least a 50–50 chance of being reelected. Many ventured that he appeared to have gained an edge over former Massachusetts governor Mitt Romney, who had emerged in April as the near-certain Republican nominee.

This represented a sharp shift in political fortune for Obama, who just a year earlier was widely viewed as the underdog for the 2012 contest. Apart from a major scandal, there are few things that can damage a first-term president's

FIGURE 1
President Obama's Job Approval

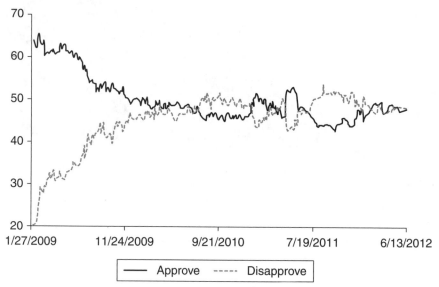

Source: Data are from the average of national polls published on the Real Clear Politics website: http://www.realclear politics.com/epolls/other/president_obama_job_approval-1044.html#polls.

popularity more than a sputtering national economy. And that was the political burden Obama faced as he approached his campaign for another four years in the White House.

Although he inherited the crisis sparked by the catastrophic bursting of the "housing bubble" during the final months of Republican predecessor George W. Bush's presidency, it was during Obama's first year as president that the recession deepened to the nation's worst since the Great Depression. Unemployment topped off at 10 percent in October 2009, nine months after he was sworn into office, and it remained stubbornly high for many months after.

Obama pushed several measures to stem the downturn, including hundreds of billions of dollars in federal "stimulus" spending and extensions of the federal "bail-outs" of the banking, investment, and automobile industries that were initiated under Bush. But these actions provoked a political backlash, amplified by the rapid rise of a conservative movement known as the Tea Party.

Despite the roiled political environment, Obama and the Congress then controlled by fellow Democrats pressed ahead with key items on their progressive political agenda, most prominently a complicated overhaul of the nation's health insurance system to expand coverage, enacted in May 2010, that was easy for Republicans to attack and very difficult for Democrats to explain and defend. The November 2010 midterm elections proved disastrous for Democrats, leaving Obama during the second two years of his term to deal with a House of Representatives controlled by conservative Republicans determined to challenge the president and a Senate in which Democrats were trimmed back to a narrow majority.

But like some other recent presidents who struggled during their first two years in office—including Republican Ronald Reagan in the 1980s and Democrat Bill Clinton in the 1990s—Obama enjoyed some positive developments in the run-up to his reelection campaign. The economy, which had continued to stumble for nearly two years after the statistical end of the recession in June 2009, finally showed signs of a steady if unspectacular recovery, and the national unemployment rate trended downward to 8.1 percent by April 2012 before ticking back up to 8.2 percent in May. An aggressive effort led by House Republicans to push a conservative agenda, which included deep cuts in government spending and a staunch opposition to tax increases even on the wealthiest Americans, abetted Obama's effort to reposition himself as a voice of moderation and reason who was more in tune with the concerns of middle-class Americans.

On the international front, Obama gained unprecedented stature in May 2011, when he authorized the raid in Pakistan by a team of U.S. Navy Seals that resulted in the shooting and death of the al Qaeda leader Osama bin Laden, the instigator of the September 11, 2001, terrorist attacks on the United States. And while a U.S. military engagement in a deadly standoff with Islamist radicals in Afghanistan passed its ten-year mark in late 2011, Obama completed a withdrawal of U.S. combat troops from Iraq, ending a commitment begun by Bush in 2003 that had grown highly unpopular.

The Republicans, meanwhile, engaged in a bruising, months-long battle over which candidate would win the nomination to challenge Obama. Romney was the consensus front-runner at the beginning of the campaign, based on his 2002 win for governor as a Republican in heavily Democratic Massachusetts and the vast personal wealth he had amassed as a venture capitalist and corporate takeover specialist. But the Republican voting base is very conservative, and though Romney professes a conservative agenda, he had difficulty persuading voters on the right that he was truly one of them—in part because he once supported abortion rights and gay rights and, as governor, signed into law a health care overhaul for Massachusetts that many observers describe (over Romney's strong objections) as the model for the Obama plan that Republican partisans widely loathe.

Romney had a huge fund-raising edge; he was backed by the best-financed "Super PAC" (Super political action committee), which slammed his opponents with millions of dollars in negative advertising; and the once-crowded field of competitors narrowed to three, each with considerable flaws: former Pennsylvania senator Rick Santorum, an outspoken and at times controversial social conservative, who had lost his 2006 contest for Senate reelection by a 17-percentage point margin; former Georgia representative Newt Gingrich, who was ousted as House Speaker by fellow Republicans in 1998, just four years after he masterminded the midterm election campaign that boosted the party to the majority; and Texas representative Ron Paul, whose iconoclastic conservative libertarian philosophy drew him a fervent but quite small following.

Nonetheless a series of narrow victories and losses for Romney stretched the contest out for weeks, and there was speculation that no candidate would earn a majority of delegates, leaving it up to the Republican National Convention in Tampa in late August to determine the nominee. It was not until April that Romney gained the appearance of true inevitability, as lead rival Santorum—trailing in the delegate count and forced to leave the campaign trail because of a young daughter's health issues—quit the race. Even at that point, grassroots efforts by Paul's supporters produced victories at Republican conventions in states such as Nevada and Maine that will guarantee the dissident candidate a delegate presence at the convention.

Yet even though Romney began the general election contest against Obama with weak approval ratings and political wounds, some of them self-inflicted by verbal gaffes, a serious challenge to the incumbent could not be ruled out. The nation remains closely divided in partisan and ideological terms, as it has been for many years. The vast majority of Republicans are implacably opposed to Obama, which is likely to keep the general election contest competitive regardless of whether Romney runs well or poorly. And many in the crucial swing constituency of independent voters remain skeptical of the president.

At the least Obama has a bit more of a cushion from the previous election than most recent predecessors who sought a second term. Obama's 53 percent vote share (to 46 percent for Arizona senator John McCain, the Republican nominee) was the first clear popular vote majority for a presidential winner since Republican George H.W. Bush received the same number in his 1988 victory over Democrat Michael S. Dukakis.

Obama's 365 electoral votes in 2008 were 94 more than he needed for a bare majority. He could still eke out a narrow victory in 2012 even if he were to lose three states where he broke long Democratic presidential losing streaks in 2008—North Carolina (15 electoral votes), Virginia (13), and Indiana (11)—and lose the key swing states of Florida (29) and Ohio (18), but only if he were able to carry every other state he carried four years ago.

As of June 2012 that still appeared a very big IF. So much would depend on whether the improvement in the economy continued unabated and whether it is strong enough by November for most voters to deem Obama worthy of a second term.

Prelude to 2012: A Wildly Swinging Political Pendulum

2008: Obama, Democrats Dominate but Inherit an Economic Crisis

The political environment that Obama confronted coming into the 2012 campaign contrasted dramatically with the one in which he ran for president and won in 2008. The Democrats at that juncture, just four years earlier, appeared to be building strong and sustainable momentum, and the Republicans—in a shambles, mainly because of the sharp decline in Bush's popularity during his second term in the White House—appeared headed toward a long period of rebuilding.

MAP 1
2008 Electoral Vote

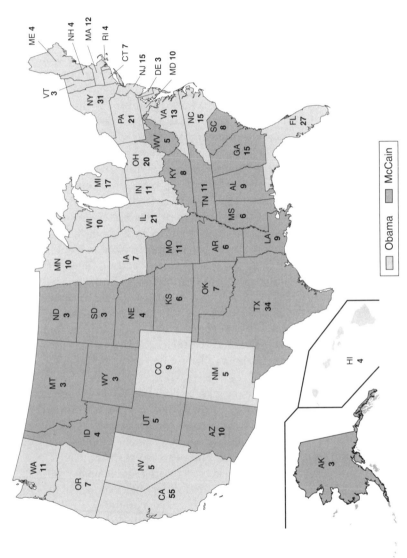

Note: Nebraska's electoral votes were divided four for McCain and one for Obama. It is one of only two states that is not statewide winner take all, but rather allots three of its five electoral votes based on the outcomes in each of the three congressional districts. Obama's campaign targeted the 2nd District, which includes Omaha, and produced a big turnout that enabled him to carry the district and win its electoral vote.

Bush's presidency was enmeshed in controversy from its very beginnings. Ballot counting controversies in the decisive state of Florida delayed the outcome of the November 2000 contest between Bush and Democrat Al Gore, then the vice president of the United States, for a month, until a 5–4 decision by the U.S. Supreme Court terminated the recounts and allowed the certification of Bush's hair-thin victory margin to stand.

Bush briefly gained strong support across party lines with his assertive response to the September 2001 terrorist attacks, which included his initiation of a U.S. military intervention in Afghanistan to remove the radical Taliban government that had harbored bin Laden and al Qaeda.

But deep political divisions returned as the Bush administration took a confrontational approach to Democratic opponents in Congress; aggressively (and successfully) pushed for the Republicans to win a majority of seats in the Senate in the 2002 elections and regain complete control of Congress; and, most important, insisted that Congress, just before the 2002 midterm elections, approve a resolution authorizing military action to remove the regime of the Iraq dictator Saddam Hussein.

Most Americans initially supported Bush's decision to launch a U.S.-dominated invasion of Iraq in March 2003. Bush and his advisers used as their leading rationale that Iraq was stockpiling weapons of mass destruction, possibly including components for nuclear weapons, and promised that any military action would be swift with minimal loss of American lives.

But Iraq ultimately contributed greatly to the undoing of Bush's and his party's political standing. Though Hussein was quickly ousted (he would be captured that December and hanged by the successor Iraqi government three years later), an extensive search uncovered no stores of weapons of mass destruction. The removal of Hussein's iron-fisted rule also unleashed the furies of sectarian violence, with American armed forces, their role altered to pacification and nation-building, caught in the middle.

Despite rapidly declining approval ratings, Bush did narrowly win reelection in 2004, aided by a period of economic growth and a lackluster campaign by Massachusetts senator John Kerry, the Democratic challenger. But support for Bush went into free fall in the aftermath of the federal government's stumbling response to devastation inflicted on New Orleans and other areas of the Gulf Coast by Hurricane Katrina in August 2005. Democratic activists got fired up to punish Bush and his GOP allies, while many conservatives in the Republican rank and file grumbled about a rising tide of federal debt that had occurred on Bush's watch.

These factors fueled a successful push by Democrats to reclaim control of Congress in the 2006 elections with a 30-seat gain in the House and a 6-seat gain in the Senate. Democrats appeared to have a golden opportunity to win the White House in 2008 that grew as the decade's economic boom—fueled heavily by large amounts of government spending and personal debt, much of that in mortgage loans that had produced a sharp run-up in the housing market—began to sputter.

The early front-runner for the Democratic nomination was Hillary Rodham Clinton, the former first lady of the United States, who had won a Senate seat from

New York in 2000 as husband Bill Clinton was completing his eight-year tenure as president. Clinton emphasized her experience at the epicenter of American politics and the historic potential of her strong bid to become the nation's first woman president.

But Clinton was seriously challenged and then overtaken by Obama early in the Democratic nominating campaign. It was only in 2004 that Obama had risen from obscurity as a state senator in Illinois by making a stirring keynote address at that year's Democratic convention and then winning a seat in the U.S. Senate. His skill at inspirational rhetoric drew him a huge following in 2008, a year when many Americans were disillusioned by the direction of the country and the stewardship of the nation's political establishment.

Although Obama's progressive agenda pleased most Democrats and a number of independents, his appeal was rooted more in the aspirational tone of his campaign than in specific policy proposals. His slogan was "Yes, We Can." His themes were hope and change, and among the things he promised to change was the bitter partisan divide that had contributed to policy gridlock in Washington. And his bid to break the nation's most profound racial barrier by becoming the first African American president proved highly motivating to black voters and most young people across racial lines.

Although Obama maintained a steady lead over the Republicans' chosen candidate, veteran Arizona senator John McCain, a Democratic victory was not a done deal heading into the fall campaign. McCain's surprise vice-presidential choice of Alaska governor Sarah Palin, a dynamic but controversial conservative ideologue, thrilled much of the dispirited Republican voting base, though she ultimately alienated many voters in the crucial constituency of "swing" voters.

The last straw, though, came in September, when what had been a gradual economic downturn turned into a major crisis. Billions of dollars in bad mortgage investments threatened banks and investment companies with complete collapse until Bush negotiated a federal rescue plan with congressional Democrats (which was enacted over the strong objections of many conservative Republicans). The unemployment rate, which stood at 5 percent when the election year began, climbed to 6.8 percent by November.

This potent reminder of what many Americans had come to view as Bush's failed leadership boosted Obama, who went on to defeat McCain by 53 to 46 percent in the popular vote and by 365 to 173 in the electoral college. The strength of the Democratic surge helped the party pad its congressional majorities by another 7 seats in the Senate and by 21 seats in the House.

Democratic Agenda Prompts Conservative "Tea Party" Backlash

Although a close partisan divide in the American electorate had already produced repeated swings in the nation's political pendulum, there is always a powerful temptation for the party that prevails in an election to interpret its success as a mandate for its agenda rather than mainly a rejection of the opposition party.

Obama takes the oath of office, administered by Chief Justice John Roberts, at the U.S. Capitol on January 20, 2009. The high-minded tone of his 2008 campaign and the relief most voters expressed at the end of George W. Bush's presidency earned Obama the approval of two-thirds of those who responded to polls at the start of his tenure.

The Democrats, having gained control of the White House and both chambers of Congress simultaneously for the first time since the 1994 elections, pressed ahead on their top priorities in the areas of economic, health care, and environmental policies. But they quickly faced dissent from many people who viewed them as pushing too far and too fast and accused them of failing to focus sufficient attention on what had become the worst recession in eight decades.

After running a campaign in which he pledged to try to achieve bipartisan solutions in Washington, Obama declined to lay blame on Bush and other Republicans for the nation's worsening economic condition. He made some concessions on his first major legislative initiative, a spending measure named the American Recovery and Reinvestment Act that was aimed at stemming the downturn and stimulating an economic recovery. About a third of the total cost was in the form of temporary tax cuts for most Americans, and the total price tag of a bit more than $800 billion disappointed many liberals in the Democratic base who argued that a much bigger package was needed to put people back to work and regenerate growth.

Yet Obama soon discovered that he and his party were on their own. Despite their consecutive setbacks at the polls, Republican congressional leaders managed to instill remarkable party unity in their attempts to hold the line against the Democratic majorities. The stimulus legislation passed over the unanimous opposition of Republicans in the House and with the support of only 3 of the 41 Republicans in the Senate. The lack of Republican fingerprints on the measure would be used to bolster the party's arguments that it was a budget-busting boondoggle, as the economy continued to decline sharply until the summer of 2009, and the unemployment rate, up to 7.3 percent already that January when Obama took over from Bush, topped off at 10 percent that October.

The efforts by conservative Republicans (who made up most of the party's ranks in Congress) to push back against Obama soon received a strong boost with the rise, beginning in the early spring of 2009, of a loosely organized but potent backlash movement that adopted the label of the Tea Party, after the famed Boston protest by American colonists against arbitrary British rule in 1773. The Tea Party activists emboldened Republican policymakers who had already dug in their heels against Obama. But they also were demanding, threatening to foment primary challenges against members of the Republican Party establishment who deviated at all from conservative doctrine—a posture that would have both positive and negative consequences for the GOP in the 2010 midterm elections and the run-up to 2012.

One of the earliest impacts of the Tea Party phenomenon was the decision by the six-term Pennsylvania senator Arlen Specter, one of the few remaining old-school moderates in the Republican congressional ranks, to switch to the Democratic Party to avoid a threatening GOP primary challenge in 2010 by a more conservative candidate. The move was initially seen as another sign of the Democrats' surge, as it temporarily gave them 60 seats in the Senate—the so-called filibuster-proof majority, as 60 votes are needed in the Senate to cut off debate and move to a vote in which a simple majority can pass legislation.

But the switch ultimately failed to salvage Specter's reelection bid. He lost the Pennsylvania primary the following May to Rep. Joe Sestak, a more liberal Democrat who would go on to narrowly lose the general election to conservative Republican Patrick J. Toomey.

And more broadly, the Democrats' majority proved more filibuster-proof in theory than practice, as some of the party's more moderate to conservative senators, along with some others who appeared vulnerable in their 2010 reelection bids, hesitated to support some of the more controversial aspects of Obama's agenda.

This became painfully evident to Democrats early on. Obama had promised in 2008 to address growing public concerns about global climate change, a position that appeared in polls to have a great deal of public support. But the legislative solution he proposed in 2009—the centerpiece of which was a "cap-and-trade" plan that would have placed overall limits on "greenhouse gases" while allowing a trading market in emissions credits—was immediately portrayed as the equivalent of a job-killing energy tax that would further damage an already ailing economy. The bill narrowly passed the House with key votes from some incumbents from politically competitive swing districts, some of whom subsequently expressed anger about being left out on a limb when the Democrats in the Senate failed to break a Republican filibuster and shelved the bill.

The inspirational rhetoric that Obama employed during his 2008 election campaign had a downside after he took office. It created high expectations that became difficult for him to meet as a president beset by major problems and faced with stiff resistance from the opposition Republican Party from his first day in office.

But no issue besides the overall economy set the tone for the 2010 elections, giving Republicans added momentum and putting Democrats on the defensive, more than the health insurance overhaul legislation that Republicans (and much of the media) labeled as "Obamacare."

Obama and congressional Democratic leaders sought to offset concerns that their proposal would create a big new federal entitlement program. They quickly dismissed a single-payer government-run plan and then took off the table a "public option"—essentially a government-run insurance company that would provide more affordable premiums to the uninsured than were available in the private market—even though that move angered many in the party's liberal base.

The proposal maintained the structure of the private-sector health insurance industry while requiring certain benefits, such as barring companies from refusing coverage for individuals with preexisting conditions and allowing parents to include children up to twenty-six years of age in their plans. But Republicans branded the measure as a "government takeover" of the health insurance system and focused much of their criticism on one major element of the legislation: the "individual mandate," which would require all Americans to either purchase health insurance, individually or through group plans, or participate in government-assisted risk pools known as insurance exchanges; or beginning in 2015, pay a penalty that would go toward offsetting government outlays for the program. Opponents said that this provision unconstitutionally exceeded the federal government's authority to regulate commerce by requiring individuals to purchase a commercial product, whether they wanted to or not.

With Republicans united in opposition, some of the more conservative Democrats concerned about certain provisions, and politically vulnerable Democratic incumbents worried about the political impact of the health care bill in the 2010 midterm elections, the congressional debates dragged on for months until Obama and Democratic leaders in Congress nailed down enough votes to narrowly pass the bill in the House. Polls through the remainder of the election year consistently showed that more Americans opposed than supported the new law.

2010: Republicans Take Back the House, Trim Democrats' Senate Edge

Big swings in national elections require that at least some percentage of voters switch their party preference from the last time they went to the polls. But there is a factor that is at least as important, and probably more so: a phenomenon labeled as the "enthusiasm gap," in which the die-hard supporters of one party are more driven to turn out and vote than the usually loyal base of the opposite party.

The enthusiasm gap benefited Democrats in the 2006 and 2008 election cycles, when the travails of Bush's second term fired up their voting base and left Republican dispirited. But the gap was reversed emphatically in 2010.

Republican voters, many of whom had strongly opposed Obama's election two years earlier, turned out in force. Meanwhile, many people who were strongly inclined to favor Democrats nonetheless expressed disappointment that Obama had not delivered on all of his promises to unify the nation behind a program of progressive change, even though the president's latitude was constricted by the nation's struggling economy and by a Republican opposition determined not to give him an inch.

Exit polls taken during the November 2010 voting showed a particularly big drop-off among two groups—African Americans and the youngest cohort of eligible voters (eighteen to twenty-four years old)—who were among the most inspired by Obama's rhetoric and persona in 2008 and had turned out in much above normal numbers to help elect him as president.

A huge upset win in a January Senate special election in Massachusetts provided the biggest early signal that 2010 could be a strong comeback year for the Republicans. The Democrats had been heavily favored to hold the seat left vacant by the August 2009 death of liberal icon Edward M. Kennedy, because of Massachusetts's long-standing Democratic leanings and because of sentiment toward the Kennedy family, which included the late president John F. Kennedy and the late New York senator Robert F. Kennedy. But both the national Republican Party establishment and the Tea Party movement leaders, sensing an opportunity to strike a blow against Obama

Republican John A. Boehner of Ohio accepts the gavel representing his new position of U.S. House Speaker from his predecessor, Democrat Nancy Pelosi of California, as the 112th Congress convened on January 5, 2011. Pelosi, who had been Speaker for four years, resumed the role of minority leader that she held from 2003 to 2007 and which Boehner held for four years prior to the Republicans' big comeback in the 2010 elections.

and his controversial health care plan, rallied behind Republican Scott P. Brown, a previously little-known state senator, who also benefited from campaign stumbles committed by the Democratic nominee, state attorney general Martha Coakley.

Another major event in January 2010 also would have important consequences in the fall campaigns. The Supreme Court, by a 5–4 vote in the case of *Citizens United v. Federal Election Commission*, struck down a provision of the 2002 Bipartisan Campaign Reform Act that barred corporations and unions from running political ads within 60 days of a general election and 30 days of a primary, with the narrow majority declaring it an unconstitutional infringement on freedom of speech. The ruling established as a matter of law that corporate entities have free speech rights equivalent to those of individuals.

The ruling prompted the rise of a new variety of political action committee, labeled Super PACs, which could accept unlimited amounts of money from wealthy individuals, businesses, and unions and use those funds on "independent expenditure" advertising campaigns to abet the election of favored candidates (as long as the PACs had no direct ties or communications with those candidates' campaigns). And while Obama and fellow Democrats initially focused on what would be an unsuccessful effort to enact legislation to strictly regulate Super PACs, Republicans plunged in to establish several major committees, including American Crossroads, a group with major political players who included Karl Rove, the longtime political adviser to George W. Bush, and Ed Gillespie, a former chief of staff to Bush who also formerly chaired the Republican National Committee. The Republicans' head start on Super PACs at the least helped reinforce the party's momentum in the 2010 congressional elections.

The Tea Party movement helped build and sustain the energy behind the backlash against Obama and Democratic control of Congress, but its demands that Republicans adhere to its doctrinaire conservative agenda ended up as less than an unalloyed blessing for the party. It appeared to contribute to the momentum that enabled the Republicans to reclaim a majority in the House with a stunning 63-seat net gain and also played a role in the 6-seat net gain that cut the Democrats' Senate majority from 59 to 53 seats. But the victories of hard-line, Tea Party-backed candidates who challenged the favorites of the Republican establishment proved hollow in key races in Nevada, Colorado, and Delaware, as the Democratic candidates succeeded in branding their opponents as too radical.

Obama's Appeal Sags, but Voters Weary of GOP Confrontation

The huge setback suffered by the Democrats left Obama in a defensive position as the 112th Congress convened in January 2011. While his party eked out enough victories to maintain a Senate majority that would be able to block any sweeping conservative policy initiatives, it also was clear that the president would face an adversarial and confrontational relationship with a Republican-controlled House that included a number of freshman members who had either emerged from the Tea Party movement or had run with its stated support.

But the tendency for a winning party to push beyond the public's comfort zone—which the Democrats themselves had exhibited during their brief four-year period of congressional control—quickly eroded the Republicans' momentum and helped Obama regain his political footing in the months before the 2012 presidential campaign began in earnest.

Public opinion polls suggested strongly that the outcome of the 2010 elections had more to do with anger aimed at the Democrats over the weak economy and the health care law than a warm embrace of the Republicans' conservative agenda. A CNN-Opinion Research poll conducted in mid-December 2010, a little more than a month after the Republicans had made their big gains, showed that 47 percent of respondents had a favorable impression of the Democratic Party compared with 42 percent who felt that way about the Republicans.

The Republican leadership in the House, which included Speaker John A. Boehner of Ohio and Majority Leader Eric Cantor of Virginia, nonetheless pushed aggressively to set its own policy agenda, demanding deep and immediate cuts in federal spending—with domestic, nonmilitary programs targeted for nearly all of the reductions—and, for the most part, rejecting any tax increases as part of a program to reduce the escalation in the national debt.

In doing so, the party appeared to walk into the same "mandate trap" that had hurt the Democrats politically after they rose to power on a wave of dissatisfaction with Bush.

The Republicans did win some battles during the first year of the 112th Congress in their efforts to force Democrats to concede that some significant spending cuts would be in order to rein in annual federal budget deficits that had ballooned to more than $1 trillion. But Republicans dug in their heels, and their approach provoked a pushback by Obama and congressional Democrats.

The parties staged pitched battles in spring 2011 over a much-delayed spending bill for the remainder of that fiscal year. This threatened for a time to cause a shutdown of nonessential federal government operations. Republicans ultimately agreed to a measure that would cut about $40 billion from the federal budget but made it clear that they regarded this as a small down payment on bigger cuts.

Obama and Republican leaders, most prominently Boehner, held negotiations on a possible "grand bargain" that would have not only mainly featured spending reductions but also included some tax increases. This effort fell through, with plenty of finger-pointing.

The possibility of a bipartisan agreement to deeply cut the budget deficit got another airing midyear after Republicans balked at raising the federal debt ceiling, a long-routine procedure to enable the government to borrow more money to pay for its commitments. Although Obama administration officials and many economists warned that failing to raise the debt ceiling would cause a default that would greatly damage the nation's creditworthiness and impede the fragile economic recovery, House Republicans only agreed to an increase in August after the White House committed to $2.4 trillion in deficit reduction over ten years.

How those reductions were going to be made was left uncertain, though, when a bipartisan congressional "supercommittee" tasked with reaching a deal broke down along party lines and stalemated in late November 2011.

Meanwhile the fluid nature of the resentments expressed by much of the public began to erode what advantages the Republicans held.

In 2010 much of that anger centered on the actions of government, particularly so-called big government solutions that most dissenting voters associated with Obama and the Democratic Party. The financial assistance programs—or "bailouts"—that were launched under Bush in 2008 to prevent the collapse of investment firms, banks, and the domestic auto companies, and sustained by Obama, were subject of populist outrage, as was the Obama health care initiative, which Republican critics portrayed as a vast expansion of the federal government's regulatory reach.

But some of that grassroots, middle-class anger also began to shift to the wealthy, who many people believed had walked away unscathed, or even benefited financially, while millions of Americans lost their jobs and their homes.

The catalyst came from the left-wing counterculture, which in autumn 2011 produced the "Occupy Wall Street" movement. Beginning with an encampment in a park in New York City's financial district, protesters in many cities across the nation vented about the growing wealth gap between the richest 1 percent and the vast majority of Americans.

The scruffiness of many Occupy activists initially encouraged conservatives to try to brand it as a revival of the drug-infused hippie culture of the 1960s. But the central message of economic equity promoted by the Occupy movement hit home with many people. A poll taken December 7 through 11, 2011, by the Pew Research Center for the People and the Press found that 29 percent of respondents approved of the Occupy movement's tactics, while 49 percent disapproved. Yet when asked about the concerns raised by the Occupy protests, 48 percent said they agreed, while 30 percent said they disagreed.

Protesters aligned with the nascent Occupy Wall Street movement, which focused on the increasing concentration of wealth in the hands of the richest 1 percent of Americans, marched in New York City on November 17, 2011. The "Occupy" label spread to protests in numerous other U.S. cities.

With Republicans in Congress plunging ahead in pursuit of conservative goals and Democrats pushing back hard, public approval for Congress fell to record lows. Five major polls conducted early- to mid-January of 2012 showed approval of Congress's job performance (Figure 2) in a range between 11 and 13 percent—slightly better than the 9 percent reported in a CBS News poll in early November.

The final partisan confrontation of 2011 had come in December, and it was one in which Obama and his fellow Democrats appeared to gain an unusually clear political advantage.

A Social Security payroll tax reduction that had been part of Obama's program to try to stimulate the economy was due to expire at the end of the year. When it became clear that agreement on how to pay for a long-term extension could not be reached

FIGURE 2
Congressional Job Approval

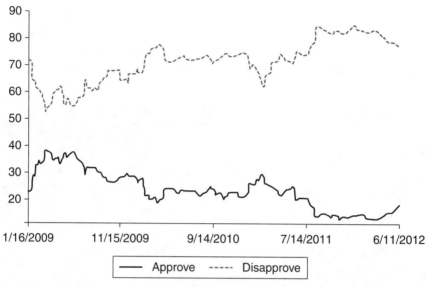

Source: Data are from the average of national polls published on the Real Clear Politics website: http://www
.realclearpolitics.com/epolls/other/congressional_job_approval-903.html#polls.

before that date, Obama and Senate Republican leaders agreed on a two-month extension of the payroll tax break, but House Republicans rejected the plan.

The showdown enabled Obama to take advantage of what has long been known
as a president's "bully pulpit." He made a surprise visit to the White House press
room on December 20 to accuse a "faction" of House Republicans of stalling tactics
that threatened 160 million Americans with a tax increase eleven days later.

The House Republicans' stance proved problematic. Some Republicans worried
that the House majority, which staunchly opposed efforts to raise taxes on the
wealthiest Americans, was picking the wrong fight on a tax issue that affected most
of the nation's workers.

Boehner and the other House Republican leaders ended up yielding and an extension was approved, but not before political damage was done. As the conservative
columnist Charles Krauthammer wrote on December 23, 2011, in *The Washington
Post*,

> The Democrats set a trap and the Republicans walked right into it. By rejecting
> an ostensibly bipartisan "compromise," the Republican House was portrayed
> as obstructionist and, even worse, heartless—willing to raise taxes on the
> middle class while resolutely opposing any tax increases on the rich.

The incident also underscored the most tangible impact of the left-wing Occupy Wall Street movement that had arisen during the previous fall—an increase in the amount of national attention paid to the issue of income inequality in America.

By the end of 2011 the physical presence of Occupy had diminished, as authorities in several cities moved aggressively to clear its encampments, and others dwindled with the onset of wintry weather. But as the *New York Times* reported after the original Wall Street protest was dispersed, "Whatever the long-term effects of the Occupy movement, protesters have succeeded in implanting 'We are the 99 percent,' referring to the vast majority of Americans . . . into the cultural and political lexicon."

The Republican Nominating Campaign's Long and Winding Road

Voters' Lukewarm Reception for Front-Runner Romney

While Obama was battling back from the lowest point of his term, the Republican contest to choose a nominee to challenge him was turning into a muddle. Despite Obama's apparent vulnerability, several prominent Republicans who had been heavily lobbied by supporters to run in 2012 decided not to enter the race.

They included Palin, the 2008 Republican vice-presidential nominee. Palin abruptly resigned as governor of Alaska in July 2009, just two and a half years into her term, but remained in the national spotlight as the author of two autobiographical books that featured her conservative views, as a political commentator on the right-leaning Fox News Channel, and even as the star of a reality television show about her life as a working mother and outdoorswoman in rough-hewn Alaska. But her new roles also provided her with lucrative career opportunities, and she and other family members chafed at life in the political fishbowl, facing criticisms that were quite personal as well as political. After leaving open questions about her intentions, Palin announced in October 2011 that she would not enter the race but would continue to try to influence national policy from the outside.

Other Republicans who were touted as potentially strong challengers, but demurred, included Jeb Bush, the retired two-term governor of Florida and the son and brother of presidents named George Bush; Mitch Daniels, who in 2008 had swum against the national Democratic tide by easily winning election to a second term as governor of Indiana, a key presidential swing state; and Chris Christie, who had quickly gained national attention after winning the 2009 governor's race in normally Democratic-leaning New Jersey with his brusque efforts to reduce state spending and challenge government employees' unions.

Their decisions to not run left Romney as the consensus front-runner for the Republican nomination, if a bit by default. Though Romney's bid to be the 2008 Republican nominee had fallen well short, he resumed his efforts to build a national base shortly after McCain was defeated that November by Obama, and he entered the 2012 race with a number of political assets.

Mitt Romney speaks at the Iowa State Fair in Des Moines on August 11, 2011, during the early stages of his campaign for the Republican presidential nomination. It was at this appearance that Romney—who made several remarks during the campaign that drew attention to his personal wealth—responded to a heckler with the statement, "Corporations are people, my friend."

Romney's success at winning the 2002 race for governor of Massachusetts provided the basis of the argument that he would be better suited than most Republicans at competing in other states that typically lean Democratic. His successful tenure as cofounder and chief executive officer of Bain Capital, a Boston-based private equity firm best known for its corporate takeover and reorganization efforts, underscored his contention that the nation needed a president with a serious business background to fix the troubled economy and also gave him substantial wealth—he has stated his net worth is about $150 million—that he could employ to help fund his campaign if he chose to do so. He also is remembered for stepping in to head and successfully stage the Winter Olympic Games held in Salt Lake City, Utah, in early 2002 after the event was put at risk by financial scandals.

But Romney also had some issues that undermined his 2008 bid and would arise again, even as he sought to project an image of inevitability in a field of Republican candidates that, at its maximum, grew to eight other candidates who were regularly invited to the first televised debates during the summer of 2011: Santorum, Gingrich, Paul, Texas governor Rick Perry, Minnesota representative Michele Bachmann, businessman Herman Cain, former Utah governor Jon Huntsman Jr., and former Minnesota governor Tim Pawlenty.

Romney's biggest problem in securing a critical mass of support in Republican primaries and caucuses was an enduring suspicion among many staunchly conservative voters that he did not stand as far to the right as he had positioned himself. His first political venture was a 1994 challenge to Massachusetts senator Edward M. Kennedy, and Romney in that campaign professed to be a supporter of abortion and gay rights, positions he said he altered in intervening years as he learned more about the issues. When he ran for governor in 2002, he cast himself as a conservative who would be willing and able to negotiate with the Democrats who thoroughly dominated the Massachusetts legislature.

Perhaps the biggest obstacle Romney faced in appealing to the Republican base was the fact that the landmark achievement of his four-year tenure as governor was shaping and signing into law a sweeping overhaul of the Massachusetts health insurance system. The plan included an individual mandate, meaning that most of the state's citizens would be required to purchase health care coverage, either independently or through employer-provided insurance plans, with lower-income residents provided with means-tested government assistance to procure insurance.

Romney on April 12, 2006, signed legislation overhauling Massachusetts's health insurance system, with Sen. Edward M. Kennedy, a longtime liberal advocate of health care reform, looking over his left shoulder. As a 2012 presidential candidate, Romney denied allusions by many Democrats, Republican opponents, and a number of independent analysts that his state law was a model for President Obama's health insurance overhaul, which Romney said he would repeal.

These provisions prompted Romney's Republican rivals for the nomination to brand the Massachusetts program as "Romneycare" and portray it as the model for the controversial federal legislation that they called "Obamacare." Democrats, seeking to make the campaign more difficult for Romney, concurred with that view and also accused Romney of hypocrisy for pledging to repeal and replace the health care measure that Obama had signed into law. But Romney denied that either was the case, stating that the program he had instituted in Massachusetts was shaped to the particular needs of that state's population and could not and should not be used as the baseline for a one-size-fits-all national program.

Also discussed, though generally handled gingerly in the political and media spheres was whether Romney's Mormon religion would be a factor in the campaign. In particular many evangelical Christians, who make up a substantial portion of the Republican electorate, have a history of hostility toward Mormonism because its doctrine includes its own interpretation of the Holy Scriptures.

Gaffes, Flawed Campaigns Cull Crowded Field

The doubts expressed by conservative activists led them to briefly embrace a series of alternative candidates during the early stages of the nominating campaign.

At various junctures, Romney was surpassed in polls of Republican voters by Perry, who as Bush's successor as Texas governor had targeted his appeal strongly to the party's conservative activist wing; Cain, a flamboyant businessman and the only African American candidate in the field, who drew attention for his potential as a strongly conservative counterweight to Obama; Gingrich, who maintained some appeal as the leader of the "Republican revolution" of the early 1990s and as someone who takes an unusually intellectual approach to political combat; and Santorum, who emerged from the back of the pack and made a timely surge, just as voting was getting under way, behind a wave of support from social conservatives. There also was a boomlet of interest in Bachmann, who had gained a following and media attention soon after her election to Congress in 2006 by portraying Democrats as holding extreme left-wing tendencies. Yet one by one these contenders fell to the wayside, with most of them damaged by gaffes and controversies.

The first out was Cain. Little known nationally when he launched his campaign, Cain—a former CEO of the Godfather's Pizza chain—had grabbed attention with his "9–9–9" plan to simplify the nation's tax codes by setting flat tax rates of 9 percent on personal income, corporate income, and sales of consumer items. Cain's negative assessment of Obama's policies was not significantly different from the other candidates, but it appeared to some to have special cogency coming from a black conservative. But Cain had already been slowed by criticisms of his economic plan—described by GOP rivals, Democrats, and many economists as flawed and simplistic—when he was hit by allegations that he had sexually harassed female colleagues while working as a restaurant industry lobbyist in the late 1990s. Though Cain denied the charges as a campaign of character assassination, he said he was acting to protect his family when he withdrew from the race in early December.

Eight Republican candidates crowded the stage for a debate at Oakland University in Auburn Hills, Mich., on November 9, 2011. From left are former Pennsylvania senator Rick Santorum, Minnesota representative Michele Bachmann, former House speaker Newt Gingrich, Romney, businessman Herman Cain, Texas governor Rick Perry (whose campaign was badly damaged by a mental lapse at this debate), Texas representative Ron Paul, and former Utah governor Jon Huntsman Jr.

Bachmann was next. Her fierce denunciations of Obama's policies had made her a favorite of the Tea Party activists, and there was media speculation that the charismatic conservative woman could emerge as the Sarah Palin of the 2012 campaign. But she committed a string of verbal gaffes. Most were innocuous, including one in which she identified New Hampshire rather than Massachusetts as the site of the initial Revolutionary War battles of Lexington and Concord. But one, involving an attack on Perry's record, did particular damage to her cause. Despite his overall image as a conservative stalwart, Perry angered some on the right in 2007 when he signed an order requiring sixth-grade girls in Texas to be vaccinated against a sexually transmitted virus known to be a cause of cervical cancer. But Bachmann, citing what a friend had told her about her family's experience, said the vaccine could cause mental retardation, a claim strongly refuted by medical authorities. Bachmann faded in the polls and dropped out in early January after drawing just 5 percent in the January 3 caucuses held in Iowa, the state where she was born.

But Perry himself didn't last much longer. His reputation as a skillful politician had enabled him to win three elections as governor of Texas, the nation's second-most populous state, but he stumbled badly on the national stage, especially in candidate debates. His campaign never recovered from a flub he made at a forum on November 9, 2011. Perry declared that he would reduce the size of the federal government by disbanding three major Cabinet departments. But after citing the Education and Commerce departments, he could not remember the third one, ending the awkward moment by saying, "Sorry. Oops." He then interjected later that he had intended to add the Energy Department to the list. After finishing fifth in Iowa with just 10 percent, Perry hoped to use the January 21 South Carolina primary to establish himself as the premier candidate of the South. But with polls showing that this strategy was failing, Perry dropped out two days before that contest.

The field had been reduced to four candidates—Paul, Santorum, Romney, and Gingrich—by the time this debate in Mesa, Ariz., was held on February 22, 2012.

Despite Setbacks, Romney Bobs to the Top

Neither these meteoric candidacies nor the more persisting challenges presented by Santorum, Gingrich, and Paul ever seriously threatened to derail Romney's pursuit of the Republican nomination. Romney had multiple factors working in his favor that ultimately enabled him to prevail.

Romney did develop a significant if less-than-overwhelming base of support, largely among voters who viewed his successful business career as an asset at a time when the nation was facing serious economic difficulties. Though polls throughout the early part of the campaign showed that he struggled to gain the favor of much more than a third of all Republican voters—and he suffered jarring setbacks by losing to Santorum in Iowa and to Gingrich in South Carolina—Romney did not endure a shift of his backers to other candidates. Most of those who said they thought Romney would be the Republicans' best choice stuck with him.

Romney's campaign was clearly the most professional and well organized among the GOP candidates, which helped him build a huge fund-raising advantage. By the end of 2011 his campaign committee had raised $56 million, more than double the $25 million raised by Paul, his nearest fund-raising rival, whose following was relatively small but fervent. On March 31 during the thick of the primary and caucus fight, Romney's total receipts had grown to $88 million, more than doubling Paul again and giving him a roughly 4–1 edge over both Gingrich and Santorum.

Romney received a huge assist from a formally independent Super PAC, Restore Our Future, which was founded in early 2011 by a group of longtime political and personal associates who supported his bid for president. Figures posted May 14 on the Open Secrets website of the nonpartisan Center for Responsive Politics showed that Restore Our Future had spent $46.5 million on political advertising to $17 million spent by Winning Our Future, a Super PAC backing Gingrich, and less than $8 million spent by the Red, White, and Blue PAC that favored Santorum. And during the competitive stage of the campaign, more than 90 percent of Restore Our Future's independent expenditures went toward a series of withering negative ads portraying Gingrich as an ethically challenged Washington influence peddler who had "tons of baggage" and Santorum as fiscally reckless during his past tenure as a senator and lacking the business and governing experience to seriously compete with Obama.

Romney ended up winning most of the primaries and caucus votes during the competitive stage of the campaign. And unlike his rivals, Romney had built enough of a support base nationally that even in states where he underperformed, he never finished lower than third place (Table 1).

It nonetheless took Romney almost four months into the campaign year to clear the field and firmly establish himself as the Republican Party's presumed nominee. Part of that was simply the result of changes that the party had made to its nominating process in an effort to persuade states to stop crowding their primaries and caucuses into the early weeks of the presidential year—a practice known as "front-loading," initiated during the 1980s that had accelerated and enabled candidates in most recent campaigns to clinch the party's nomination before spring arrived.

For the 2012 contest, Republicans reduced the delegate allotments for states that held their events before March and greatly restricted the latitude of state parties to hold winner-take-all events before April. As a result the busiest primary day of the year—dubbed Super Tuesday, as per a long-standing tradition—was held on March 6 with primaries and caucuses in ten states, compared with 2008, when Super Tuesday was held February 5 and featured contests in twenty states.

But persistent doubts held by many in the Republican base about Romney's dedication to conservative doctrine, and Romney's own awkward performance as a candidate also greatly slowed his march to victory in the race for the nomination.

Santorum, Gingrich, and other candidates argued that they were truer conservatives and hammered at Romney, in ads, campaign appearances, and debates. They described him as a flip-flopper who would be apt to try to moderate his views for the general election contest if he won the nomination. On health care they rebuffed Romney's denials that the Massachusetts health care law had inspired "Obamacare." Romney was not helped in his efforts to deflect such criticism in late March when Eric Fehrnstrom, one of his top political advisers, implied during an interview with CNN

TABLE 1

2012 Republican Primary and Caucus Results During Competitive Phase

State	Date	Winner	Margin	Second place	Third place
Iowa (caucuses)	Jan. 3	Santorum	0.1	**Romney**	Paul
New Hampshire	Jan. 10	**Romney**	16	Paul	Huntsman
South Carolina	Jan. 21	Gingrich	13	**Romney**	Santorum
Florida	Jan. 31	**Romney**	15	Gingrich	Santorum
Maine (caucuses)	Feb. 4–11	**Romney**	4	Paul	Santorum
Nevada (caucuses)	Feb. 4	**Romney**	29	Gingrich	Paul
Colorado (caucuses)	Feb. 7	Santorum	5	**Romney**	Gingrich
Minnesota (caucuses)	Feb. 7	Santorum	18	Paul	**Romney**
Arizona	Feb. 28	**Romney**	21	Santorum	Gingrich
Michigan	Feb. 28	**Romney**	3	Santorum	Paul
Washington (caucuses)	Mar. 3	**Romney**	14	Santorum	Gingrich
Alaska (caucuses)	Mar. 6	**Romney**	3	Santorum	Paul
Georgia	Mar. 6	Gingrich	21	**Romney**	Santorum
Idaho	Mar. 6	**Romney**	43	Santorum	Paul
Massachusetts	Mar. 6	**Romney**	60	Santorum	Paul
North Dakota	Mar. 6	Santorum	12	Paul	**Romney**
Ohio	Mar. 6	**Romney**	1	Santorum	Gingrich
Oklahoma	Mar. 6	Santorum	6	**Romney**	Gingrich
Tennessee	Mar. 6	Santorum	9	**Romney**	Gingrich
Vermont	Mar. 6	**Romney**	14	Paul	Santorum
Virginia	Mar. 6	**Romney**	20	Paul	
Wyoming (caucuses)	Mar. 6	**Romney**	17	Santorum	Uncommitted
Kansas (caucuses)	Mar. 10	Santorum	30	**Romney**	Gingrich
Alabama	Mar. 13	Santorum	5	Gingrich	**Romney**
Hawaii (caucuses)	Mar. 13	**Romney**	19	Santorum	Paul
Mississippi	Mar. 13	Santorum	2	Gingrich	**Romney**
Illinois	Mar. 20	**Romney**	12	Santorum	Paul
Louisiana	Mar. 24	Santorum	22	**Romney**	Gingrich
District of Columbia	Apr. 3	**Romney**	58	Paul	Gingrich
Maryland	Apr. 3	**Romney**	20	Santorum	Gingrich
Wisconsin	Apr. 3	**Romney**	7	Santorum	Paul
Connecticut	Apr. 24	**Romney**	54	Paul	Gingrich
Delaware	Apr. 24	**Romney**	29	Gingrich	Paul
New York	Apr. 24	**Romney**	48	Paul	Gingrich
Pennsylvania	Apr. 24	**Romney**	40	Santorum	Paul
Rhode Island	Apr. 24	**Romney**	39	Paul	Gingrich
Indiana	May 8	**Romney**	49	Paul	Santorum
North Carolina	May 8	**Romney**	55	Paul	Santorum
West Virginia	May 8	**Romney**	57	Santorum	Paul
Nebraska	May 15	**Romney**	57	Santorum	Paul
Oregon	May 15	**Romney**	58	Paul	Santorum
Arkansas	May 22	**Romney**	55	Paul	Santorum
Kentucky	May 22	**Romney**	54	Paul	Santorum
Texas	May 29	**Romney**	57	Paul	Santorum
California	Jun. 5	**Romney**	70	Paul	Santorum
Montana	Jun. 5	**Romney**	54	Paul	Santorum
New Jersey	Jun. 5	**Romney**	71	Paul	Santorum
New Mexico	Jun. 5	**Romney**	63	Santorum	Paul
South Dakota	Jun. 5	**Romney**	53	Paul	Santorum

Romney's efforts to rebuff opponents' allegation that he is a flip-flopper were not helped when an aide on March 21, 2012, implied that his campaign themes during the primary campaign could be altered for the general election as easily as a drawing on an Etch-a-Sketch toy.

that Romney would realign its approach and priority for a general election campaign against Obama, comparing the Romney campaign to a toy that allows drawings to be made by manipulating magnetic filings that can easily be erased. "It's almost like an Etch A Sketch. You can kind of shake it up and restart all over again," Fehrnstrom said.

And while all the Republican candidates proclaimed themselves as pro-business and pro-wealth, they argued that a year in which many Americans were facing economic difficulties was the wrong one in which to nominate one of the wealthiest people ever to run for president, someone who was born to comfort (his father, the late George W. Romney, was an auto company executive who served as governor of Michigan from 1963 to 1969) and who grew up to make the bulk of his fortune as a corporate takeover specialist. Perry, before he left the race, implied that Romney practiced "vulture capital-ism" rather than "venture capitalism," and Gingrich said, "Show me somebody who has consistently made money while losing money for workers and I'll show you someone who has undermined capitalism." They demanded that Romney release his tax returns, which Romney ultimately did in a limited manner and with reluctance (Table 2).

Romney unintentionally gave plenty of ammunition to his Republican opponents—and the Obama camp—by making a series of casual comments that had the effect of drawing attention to his wealth. These included challenging Perry during a debate to a

TABLE 2

Mitt Romney's Bumpy Road to Nomination

Date	Romney	Perry	Cain	Gingrich	Santorum
6/21/2011	24	5	9	7	4
9/13/2011	19	31	4	5	3
10/7/2011	22	16	16	9	3
11/3/2011	24	10	26	10	2
11/16/2011	21	9	19	20	2
12/9/2011	21	7	13	34	4
1/18/2012	33	7	n/a	18	15
2/16/2012	28	n/a	n/a	15	34
3/7/2012	38	n/a	n/a	14	26

Note: n/a = not available.

Source: Data are from the average of national polls published on the Real Clear Politics website.

Romney's claim to successful business experience, and most of his personal fortune, came from a career as head of a venture capital firm that conducted corporate takeovers and reorganizations. While Romney contends his efforts resulted in a net gain of jobs, the allegation that he had also endorsed job layoffs and outsourcing was one of his biggest burdens. And although all of the major Republican presidential candidates voiced strongly pro-business views, some sought to gain traction by attacking Romney as a "vulture capitalist," as this cartoon—depicting Gingrich and Perry as Occupy movement protestors—illustrates.

$10,000 bet concerning Romney's position on a health care individual mandate; a mention that his wife Ann "drives a couple of Cadillacs"; his attempts to show affinity with sports fans by relating that he had friends who owned NFL (National Football League) and NASCAR (National Association for Stock Car Auto Racing) teams; an attempt to show that he doesn't tolerate subpar service that came out, "I like to fire people"; a statement that his focus was on the economic problems of the middle class because lower-income people have a government safety net that came out, "I'm not concerned about the very poor"; and his exclamation, "Corporations are people, my friend," made in response to a campaign heckler who said taxes on corporations should be raised.

Romney also used the campaign for the primary in his birth state of Michigan in late February to reiterate his criticisms of the auto industry bailout, a position popular with conservatives in some parts of the country but ripe for exploitation by Democrats in general-election swing states in the industrial Midwest where the federal assistance program is viewed much more favorably.

Romney argues that allowing the auto companies to undergo orderly bankruptcy procedures would have allowed them to survive and recover without government aid. But Obama and other critics contend that bankruptcies in the midst of the credit crunch that accompanied the downturn would have been anything but orderly, resulting instead in liquidations that would have been disastrous to the regional and national economies. Critics mocked Romney's suggestion in a May 8 Cleveland

Santorum shakes hands with a supporter in New Hampshire on January 4, 2012, the day after he claimed an upset victory in the Iowa caucuses, the campaign's first test of candidate strength. Republican authorities in Iowa first reported that Romney edged Santorum by an 8-vote margin, but a final count showed that Santorum had scored a narrow victory.

television interview that he deserved "a lot of credit" for the auto industry's comeback because of the position that he took.

The tensions between Romney's political strengths and weaknesses were clearly at play during the early weeks of voting in the Republican nominating contests. Though a surge by Gingrich in polls taken in late 2011 was blunted by a barrage of negative ads run mainly by the Restore Our Future Super PAC, Santorum—not considered a major factor in the race up to that point—campaigned doggedly across Iowa and, just in time, caught the attention of many of the strongly conservative voters who would dominate the January 3 caucuses there. Although Santorum's narrow win in Iowa was initially reported as an 8-vote edge in favor of Romney, the impact in national media coverage was about the same: Romney was shaky, while Santorum was surging.

Romney did win the nation's first primary in New Hampshire a week later, but his 39 percent vote share in the state neighboring his own was viewed as underwhelming. Gingrich then rebounded briefly to defeat Romney by 40 to 28 percent in South Carolina on January 21, again raising questions about whether Romney's front-runner title was warranted.

It was not long, however, before the huge financial advantage enjoyed by Romney's campaign and the Super PAC backing his candidacy began to prove decisive. His victory margins were a mix of comfortable—14 percentage points over Gingrich in Florida on January 31, 20 points over Santorum in Arizona on February 28—and close, as his 3-point edge over Santorum in Michigan, also on February 28. That outcome again raised eyebrows because Michigan is the state where Romney was born and raised and where his father served as governor in the 1960s. He won six of the 10 Republican contests on March 3, Super Tuesday, but the day's biggest race was a cliff-hanger in Ohio that produced a 1-point win for Romney. He continued to show weakness in the South, with Santorum taking Oklahoma and Tennessee while Gingrich won his home state of Georgia.

Neither of the leading rivals was able to sustain momentum, though, in part because they—like other candidates who had fallen by the wayside, and sometimes Romney himself—had difficulty staying out of their own way.

Gingrich, who has seen himself as a visionary throughout a political career in which many critics found him high in self-regard, issued some controversial proposals during his campaign, including one under which public schools could save money by laying off adult janitors and instead paying children to clean the schools in order to teach them work skills, and another in which he appeared to run counter to his demands for fiscal conservatism by proposing that the United States build colonies on the moon by the year 2020.

Also Gingrich's personal life, which has included three marriages, caused him difficulties from the start in his bid to be nominee of a party in which social conservatism is a strongly stated principle. His wife Callista was a frequently referenced fixture by his side on the campaign trail, but Gingrich was compelled to respond to reports about a $500,000 revolving line of credit he and his wife had opened at the upscale jewelry retailer Tiffany's, and his second wife Marianne told ABC News just before the South Carolina primary that Gingrich in 1999 had asked for an "open marriage" at a time when he was conducting an extramarital affair with Callista, then a congressional aide.

Santorum, meanwhile, had made himself a factor in the race with his strongly stated conservative views on social issues, but his emphasis and fiery rhetoric on these matters raised serious concerns among many Republicans as to whether he would be a viable challenger to Obama among the broader general electorate in the fall.

He also faced grilling about some of his campaign statements, including a suggestion that Obama is a "snob" because he wants "everybody in America to go to college," and a statement that Obama and "Etch A Sketch" Romney were so alike as establishment candidates that voters might as well reelect the incumbent if Romney were to emerge as his challenger.

Also Santorum, who was seeking to become the nation's second Roman Catholic president, challenged the famous 1960 statement by the first, John F. Kennedy, in which he defended a separation of church and state. Santorum interpreted Kennedy as believing that "people of faith have no role in the public square" and said that position "makes me throw up."

Santorum continued to run strongly in the South, winning March 13 primaries in Mississippi and Alabama, but victories by Romney on March 20 in Illinois (by 12 points over Santorum), and in April 3 primaries in Wisconsin (5-point margin) and Maryland (20-point margin) made it more apparent that no one in the field would overtake him in the race for convention delegates.

Santorum initially insisted he would stay the course in hopes of holding Romney below the majority he would need to clinch a first-ballot nomination at the convention, scheduled to be held in Tampa August 27–30. But the hospitalization in early April of Bella Santorum, the candidate's three-year-old daughter who has a rare chromosome disorder, prompted Santorum to suspend his campaign. At first this was a temporary move, but with his campaign flagging and running out of money, Santorum announced April 10 in his home state of Pennsylvania that he was quitting the race.

Gingrich continued to insist, despite his also-ran showings in most primaries and caucuses, that he would campaign to the convention, but he signaled his intention to drop out on May 1 after Romney easily won primaries held April 24 in Pennsylvania, New York, Connecticut, Delaware, and Rhode Island. With Paul hanging in but viewed as having no plausible chance of winning the nomination, the political community and media began to address Romney as the Republicans' presumed challenger to Obama.

November Outlook: It's the Economy, Mainly

As the general election campaign began in earnest, Democrats repeated a mantra that they believed would clinch reelection for Obama: "Bin Laden is dead, and General Motors is alive." To advocates in the party, the raid Obama authorized that resulted in the death of the fugitive terrorist had ended any doubts about the president's toughness and decisiveness on national security matters. And the survival and revival of the domestic auto industry was presented both as the best evidence of the wisdom of Obama's economic policies in addressing the recession he inherited and a major flaw for Romney, who opposed the auto industry bailout.

Yet the political atmosphere remained volatile, and a close and competitive race to November was widely seen as more likely than an easy win for Obama. Polls taken from mid- to late April, as Romney was emerging as the near-certain Republican nominee, were all over the place, with Obama holding leads ranging from 4 to 9 percentage points in several polls, but statistically tied with Romney in others. The daily tracking poll conducted by the Gallup organization whipsawed wildly during this period, with Romney holding leads of up to 5 points in mid-April, Obama suddenly jumping out to a 7-point lead a week later, and the candidates back to a virtual tie by the end of the month.

Any number of items could ultimately have a major impact on the outcome of a contest this close. The political repercussions of the Supreme Court's decision on the constitutionality of the controversial health care law, expected by late June, will be closely examined. The unstable military situation in Afghanistan and tensions with Iran over that nation's efforts to develop a nuclear program created uncertainties on the international front. Romney's choice of a vice-presidential running mate, and the degree to which the Republican candidate is able to inspire enthusiasm among members of the conservative Republican base who have doubted him, could be key factors. And the tone for each party's fall campaign will be set by the Republican convention in the last week of August and the Democratic convention in Charlotte, N.C., a week later.

But barring a major, unpredicted event on either the domestic or international front, it appeared six months out from election day that the result of the presidential contest would most likely hinge on whether Obama can make an effective case for his economic stewardship.

Jobs, Jobs, Jobs

Obama's standing on the economy had improved considerably since the beginning of the year, but he still faced widespread doubts. A CBS-*New York Times* poll conducted December 5 through 7, 2011, showed that only 33 percent of respondents approved of Obama's handling of the economy. That figure improved to 44 percent in a survey conducted April 13 through 17, but more respondents (48 percent) said they disapproved.

The nation's unemployment rate of 8.1 percent in April was about a fifth lower than the peak of 10 percent hit in October 2009 and was a drop from 9 percent exactly one year earlier. But it ticked back up to 8.2 percent in May, and that figure was a full percentage point higher than the highest rate since the Great Depression for a president who won reelection: The 7.2 percent mark in November 1984, when Republican Ronald Reagan, who also endured a deep recession during the early part of his first term as president, won in a landslide.

People stood in a long line at a job fair in Portland, Ore., on March 7, 2012. Oregon's unemployment rate of 8.6 percent that month was about a half-percentage point higher than for the nation as a whole.

Job growth was 69,000 in the initial May national employment report from the U.S. Bureau of Labor Statistics (the numbers of new jobs were recalculated and upgraded in several previous months). This marked the 20th month of net job gains since the "great recession" reached its statistical end in October 2010.

Yet the figure was regarded as tepid by many economic analysts and the national media described the report with adjectives that ranged from "disappointing" to "brutal." It was no surprise when Romney and other Republicans jumped on the May report and described it as proof that Obama is not capable of producing a robust recovery.

Democrats fired back that Obama is still trying to clean up a mess created by economic policies that took effect when Bush was president and Republicans controlled both chambers of Congress. They also accused Romney of overstatements with his claim that the economy should be creating 500,000 new jobs a month—a figure rarely achieved even during past upswings—and that the national unemployment rate can and should be reduced to 4 percent, a figure last seen in 2000 during the last year of Democrat Bill Clinton's presidency and never achieved even during the height of the housing-driven boom of the Bush years.

Obama and his party hope that they can make a more effective case than they did during the 2010 midterm elections that the nation—and by extension the world, since the United States is still the biggest economic factor—would have been in much worse shape had it not been for the policies the president instituted during his first year in office. That contention clashed in November 2010 with the fact that unemployment still lingered at 9.8 percent, just a fraction below its recession high point more than a year earlier, which in turn gave Republicans ammunition for their attacks on Obama's stimulus program as an expensive bust.

With unemployment down by nearly 2 percentage points since then and a rebound on Wall Street restoring value to many Americans' recession-ravaged retirement portfolios, the Obama camp thinks it will get a more open hearing from voters than many Democratic candidates received during the 2010 midterms.

There is some division among political analysts about whether that Democratic optimism was warranted. In interviews conducted in early 2012, some said Obama did not need a further sharp reduction in unemployment rates in order to achieve reelection, as long as the numbers kept moving in the right direction.

"Even slight improvements in the economy, particularly the unemployment numbers, will be used as evidence that the economy is headed in the right direction. President Obama and other Democrats will say this is evidence that their policies are finally working," said Timothy Hagle, a political science professor at the University of Iowa, who cited an old political maxim, "The trend is your friend."

But others said the president's standing on the economy during the fall campaign will be less about employment statistics than about whether most voters personally sense that the nation is moving in the right direction.

"There's no magic number that gets President Obama reelected. People have to feel the economy getting better," said Nathan L. Gonzales, deputy editor of the Rothenberg Political Report in Washington, D.C. "Until their neighbor, cousin, and brother get jobs, the president is going to struggle to get reelected. President Obama is beyond the point where he can give another speech and reassure the American people. They have to feel it."

Inequality: Obama's Trump Card?

The Obama administration also was confronted with one of the most potentially damaging economic issues when the price of gasoline spiked in the first third of the year, the result largely of increasing demand that accompanied the improvements in the overall economy and international worries about the tensions with Iran, a major oil-producing nation. According to data published by the U.S. Energy Information Administration, the price of a gallon of regular gasoline jumped almost 20 percent from $3.30 in early January to $3.94 in early April before settling back down to $3.61 in early June.

The best possible trump card that Obama and other Democrats appeared to hold during the first half of 2012 was the widespread concern about the growing gap between the wealthiest Americans and those in the middle- and lower-income constituencies. "I think the number-one weapon of the Obama camp is the steady Republican opposition to higher taxes on millionaires," said Charles Ballard, an economics professor at Michigan State University. "They would say 'the Republicans are looking out for the fat cats; we need someone to look out for the average guy.'"

Obama has hit this issue hard in a number of ways, including his advocacy of the "Buffett Rule," a proposal by the president that would set a top tax rate of 30 percent for individuals making more than $1 million. This proposal is based on advocacy by billionaire investor Warren Buffett, who has said that the wealthiest Americans should not end up paying a lower portion of their income than do middle-class Americans—in his case, less than his secretary.

Republicans, who generally oppose tax increases as counterproductive to economic growth, however, have resisted the Buffett Rule. When the Senate's Democratic leaders pushed to end a Republican filibuster on legislation that would have imposed the rule—a move that needed 60 votes—they received 51–45 "no" votes. Only one Republican member, Susan Collins of Maine, voted in favor of the cloture motion, while only one Democrat, Mark Pryor of Arkansas, voted against it.

Democrats think Republicans could hardly have provided a more perfect foil on this issue than Romney, who made a habit of off-the-cuff remarks that reminded voters of the great wealth he achieved running a venture capital company that built up some of the companies it financed or took over, but also downsized others. "[The Democrats] would question whether Mitt Romney really helped the average citizen when he was working at Bain," Ballard said.

Health Care and the Supreme Court

The politically loaded dispute over the Patient Protection and Affordable Care Act of 2010, a.k.a. Obamacare, was expected to come to a head in June with a decision by the Supreme Court in the lawsuits seeking to overturn all or key parts of the law.

As illuminated by the oral arguments before the court held March 27 through 29, the core issue was whether the "individual mandate" provisions of the law were constitutional. The Obama administration's lawyers defended the requirement that all Americans either obtain health insurance by 2015 or pay financial penalties, saying that it was necessary to ensure that the extensions of coverage provided under

Both supporters and opponents of Obama's health care law rallied outside the Supreme Court on March 27, 2012, during oral arguments in the lawsuits that sought to overturn the entire measure or at least one of its most controversial provisions, the "individual mandate" to purchase health insurance coverage.

the law would be paid for, and describing it as part and parcel of the government's authority to impose taxes. Lawyers for the plaintiffs, which included the state of Florida and the National Federation of Independent Businesses, countered that the mandate was unconstitutional because it created a requirement that individuals buy a certain kind of commercial product (insurance policies) whether they desired to or not.

The political impact of the impending decision was unclear. It was almost certain that the ruling would dominate "the news cycle"—and thus become the big issue in the campaign—for some period after it was released. A ruling against the law would likely be portrayed in the immediate aftermath as a rebuke and setback to Obama, who had put months of effort into the crafting of the legislation and persuaded a number of congressional Democrats to cast votes in favor that came back to haunt them in the 2010 midterm elections. A ruling upholding the law would be touted by Democrats as vindication for the president.

The long-term effect on public opinion, though, would depend a great deal on how far-reaching the majority was in its decision. For instance, a court ruling to strike down the entire law would repeal not only controversial provisions, such as the individual mandate, but also others that polls show are popular, such as the requirements that insurance companies provide coverage to people with preexisting conditions and allow adult children up to twenty-six years of age to stay on their parents' insurance policies. If the parts the public generally likes were to go down along with the less-popular parts, it would put pressure on Romney and other Republicans to deliver a comprehensive alternative plan—something the party declined to do when it controlled both chambers of Congress for all but one-and-a-half years between the 1994 and 2006 elections, a period that also overlapped with the first six years of the George W. Bush presidency.

The breakdown of the vote among the nine justices would also be closely watched. The Court over the past dozen years had issued several controversial decisions, most of them expressing conservative viewpoints, by bare majorities of 5–4 votes, including the one that ended the 2000 Florida vote counting controversy in favor of Bush and the 2010 *Citizens United* ruling that opened the way for the creation of Super PACs. Another such narrow ruling on such a key case would fuel sentiment that the Court had surrendered its political independence and had become a repository of the nation's deep partisan divisions.

A *Washington Post*-ABC News poll taken in early April showed that 50 percent of respondents thought the ruling would be based on the justices' partisan political views to 40 percent who said it would be based on the law.

Avoiding Foreign Policy Tripwires

On May 1, 2012—the first anniversary of the U.S. raid that killed al-Qaeda leader Osama bin Laden—Obama took an unannounced flight to Afghanistan, where the next day local time he signed a new security agreement with the president of that embattled nation, Hamid Karzai. Obama then made a televised speech to the American people from an air base in Afghanistan in which he stated,

> I recognize that many Americans are tired of war. I will not keep Americans in harm's way a single day longer than is absolutely required for our national security. But we must finish the job we started in Afghanistan and end this war responsibly.

Republicans fumed that the president was exploiting the bin Laden anniversary for election-year political advantage. Democrats responded with reminders of the showy display in 2003 after the fall of Saddam Hussein in Iraq, when Bush donned a flight suit and flew on a Navy jet from California to the deck of an aircraft carrier where he delivered a speech in front of a banner that said, "Mission Accomplished"—years, it turned out, before the U.S. combat role in that nation's bloody internal conflict ended.

The emergence of foreign policy as a strong suit for Obama was not something that might have been anticipated during the 2008 campaign, when both Democratic

President Obama shakes hands with the Afghan leader Hamid Karzai on May 2, 2012, during a meeting in Kabul in which they signed a new strategic partnership agreement. Republicans criticized and Democrats defended the trip, which coincided with the first anniversary of the U.S. raid in Pakistan that killed terrorist Osama bin Laden, who was based in Afghanistan prior to the 9/11 attacks.

primary opponent Clinton and Republican general election nominee McCain made major issues of his lack of experience on defense and international affairs. The CBS News-*New York Times* poll taken April 14 through 17 showed 46 percent of respondents approved of his handling of foreign policy while 36 percent disapproved—a +10 rating at a time when the same poll showed him at -4 on the economy and -40 on his handling of gasoline prices.

Still Obama's advantage on international issues appeared fragile. Public support has slipped for the prolonged military commitment in Afghanistan, which has annually taken the lives of hundreds of members of the U.S. armed forces. Obama in late 2011 completed a military disengagement from Iraq and committed U.S. air power to the NATO (North Atlantic Treaty Organization) initiative to protect rebels in Libya earlier that year, an action that ultimately produced the downfall of Muammar Qadhafi. But concerns were raised at both ends of the political spectrum about ongoing tensions over efforts by Iran, a nation that has had a hostile relationship with the United States since its Islamic Revolution in 1979, to develop a nuclear program, with Republicans accusing the president of not being tough enough and liberals in the Democratic ranks worried that the nation might get drawn into yet another foreign conflict.

The Electoral Vote "Battlefield"

Barring major developments over the last six months of the campaign that turn President Obama into a runaway winner or send him to a crushing defeat, the outcome of the 2012 election looks likely to be quite close. If that is the case, then the outlines of the state-by-state race for an electoral vote majority appear clear.

As the "Battlefield" (Table 3) details, past election results show that each party has strong areas of regional strength that ensure—except in extreme adverse circumstances—that it will go into the fall campaign with a sizable foundation of electoral votes. If polls this fall suggest that the favored party is at risk of losing any of these states, it will be taken as a sign that the national election is moving strongly in the other party's direction.

For Romney and the Republicans, the base includes most of the states in the conservative South and largely rural swaths of the Midwest and Mountain West. Most analysts as of June viewed the Republicans as having a solid upper hand in these states: Alabama, Alaska, Georgia, Idaho, Kansas, Kentucky, Louisiana, Mississippi, Montana, Nebraska, North Dakota, Oklahoma, South Carolina, South Dakota, Tennessee, Texas, Utah, West Virginia, and Wyoming, which together provide 153 electoral votes.

But Obama and the Democrats start out with a cumulative edge in the states viewed as leaning strongly in their direction. The Democrats' presidential base is made up of the states of the Northeast and parts of the industrial Midwest and the West Coast, and it includes populous states with big electoral vote prizes, such as California, New York, and Illinois. Add in the other states presumed safely behind Obama—Connecticut, Delaware, Hawaii, Maine, Maryland, Massachusetts, New Jersey, Oregon, Rhode Island, Vermont, and Washington—plus the District of Columbia, and Obama appears to have a solid hold on 186 electoral votes. That is just 85 less than the bare majority he would need to claim a second term.

That, however, doesn't mean it will necessarily be easy for him to get there. His cause would be helped greatly if he can hold onto three states that he won with relative ease in 2008 but which are considered as potentially up for grabs because they have a recent history of competitive presidential elections. These include Michigan, the state where Romney was born and raised and where his father served as governor (but where he had trouble during the Republican primary campaign justifying his opposition to the auto industry bailout); Minnesota, where George W. Bush lost by narrow margins in both of his presidential contests; and New Mexico, which Bush won narrowly in 2004 after losing it narrowly in 2000.

If Obama can hold these states, he would add 31 more electoral votes to his base, bringing him to within 54 of his goal. Democratic Party optimists think he might have a shot at 21 more in two states that are generally perceived as leaning Republican: Missouri, a longtime swing state that has trended Republican in statewide politics but gave the

TABLE 3
The Presidential Election Battlefield

State	2000	2004	2008	2012 Electoral votes	Change from 2008	Year party last won
Democratic strongholds						**Last R win**
California	D +12	D +10	D +24	55		1988
Connecticut	D +18	D +10	D +22	7		1988
Delaware	D +13	D +8	D +25	3		1988
District of Columbia	D +76	D +80	D +86	3		Never
Hawaii	D +18	D +9	D +45	4		1984
Illinois	D +12	D +10	D +25	20	−1	1988
Maine	D +5	D +9	D +17	4		1988
Maryland	D +16	D +13	D +25	10		1988
Massachusetts	D +27	D +25	D +26	11	−1	1984
New Jersey	D +16	D +7	D +16	14	−1	1988
New York	D +25	D +18	D +27	29	−2	1984
Oregon	D +0.4	D +4	D +16	7		1984
Rhode Island	D +29	D +21	D +28	4		1984
Vermont	D +10	D +20	D +37	3		1988
Washington	D +6	D +7	D +17	12	1	1984
				186	**−4**	
Republican strongholds						**Last D win**
Alabama	R +15	R +26	R +22	9		1976
Alaska	R +31	R +26	R +22	3		1964
Georgia	R +13	R +17	R +5	16	1	1992
Idaho	R +41	R +38	R +25	4		1964
Kansas	R +21	R +25	R +15	6		1964
Kentucky	R +15	R +20	R +16	8		1996
Louisiana	R +8	R +15	R +19	8	−1	1996
Mississippi	R +17	R +21	R +13	6		1976
Montana	R +25	R +21	R +2	3		1992
Nebraska	R +29	R +33	R +15	5		1964
North Dakota	R +28	R +27	R +9	3		1964
Oklahoma	R +22	R +31	R +31	7		1964
South Carolina	R +16	R +17	R +9	9	1	1976
South Dakota	R +23	R +22	R +8	3		1964
Tennessee	R +4	R +14	R +15	11		1996
Texas	R +21	R +23	R +12	38	4	1976
Utah	R +41	R +46	R +28	6	1	1964
West Virginia	R +6	R +13	R +13	5		1996
Wyoming	R +40	R +40	R +32	3		1964
				153	**6**	
Potentially competitive (D win 2008)						**Last R win**
Michigan	D +5	D +3	D +16	16	−1	1988
Minnesota	D +2	D +3	D +10	10		1972
New Mexico	D +0.1	R +1	D +15	5		2004

(Continued)

State	2000	2004	2008	2012 Electoral votes	Change from 2008	Year party last won
				31	−1	
Potentially competitive (R win 2008)						**Last D win**
Arizona	R +6	R +10	R +8	11	1	1996
Missouri	R +3	R +7	R +0.1	10	−1	1996
				21	0	
Battleground "swing" states						**Last R win**
Colorado	R +8	R +5	D +9	9		2004
Florida	R +.01	R +5	D +3	29	2	2004
Indiana	R +16	R +21	D +1	11	−1	2004
Iowa	D +0.3	R +0.7	D +10	6	−1	2004
Nevada	R +5	R +4	D +12	6	1	2004
New Hampshire	R +1	D +1	D +10	4		2000
North Carolina	R +13	R +12	D +0.3	15		2004
Ohio	R +4	R +2	D +5	18	−2	2004
Pennsylvania	D +4	D +3	D +10	20	−1	1988
Virginia	R +8	R +7	D +6	13		2004
Wisconsin	D +0.2	D +0.4	D +14	10		1984
				141	−2	

Note: R = Republican; D = Democratic.

Republican nominee McCain a razor-thin edge over Obama, and Arizona, where a backlash against the state's tough crackdown on illegal immigration has some Democrats hoping they can generate an outsized turnout among Hispanic voters. Romney almost certainly needs to hold both of these states if he is to have a chance to win.

Regardless of how these middle-tier states pan out, the election's outcome will clearly be decided in the competitive races that are expected in up to eleven "battleground" states: Colorado, Florida, Indiana, Iowa, Nevada, New Hampshire, North Carolina, Ohio, Pennsylvania, Virginia, and Wisconsin. Obama carried all eleven of these states, but his victory margins over McCain ranged from as high as 14 percentage points in Wisconsin all the way down to three-tenths of a percentage point in North Carolina. And eight of the eleven states went Republican for president as recently as 2004, when they were crucial to putting Bush over the top in his closely fought reelection bid.

The states seen as most likely to flip to the Republicans this year are North Carolina, where Obama's win—the first by a Democratic presidential candidate since Jimmy Carter carried the state in 1976—provided the icing on an election he had already won elsewhere, and Indiana, which no Democrat had carried since incumbent Lyndon B. Johnson in 1964, until Obama eked out a win by just less than 1 percentage point.

At the other end of this group of electorally crucial states are two that seem anomalies on this list. Wisconsin last went Republican for president in 1984, and Pennsylvania last did in 1988. Both states went for Obama by double-digit percentages in 2008. But both states went Democratic only narrowly in both 2000 and 2004, and economic problems during the downturn sparked a Republican resurgence in both states during the 2010 midterm elections. Wisconsin, in particular, has already been a partisan hotbed this year, as first-term Republican governor Scott Walker survived a June 5 recall election fomented by Democrats and organized labor leaders angered by his aggressive efforts after taking office to restrict the collective bargaining rights of state workers.

These battleground states should expect frequent visits from both of the major party nominees, and their airwaves will be absolutely saturated with ads run by the candidates' campaigns, the national and state party organizations, Super PACs, and more traditional outside interest groups.

As always, the outcome of the election will be determined by which party is better able to turn out its supporters to vote. And as has been the case for many years, independents—those who choose not to affiliate with either the Republicans or the Democrats—will be courted as the voters who potentially could swing the outcome one way or the other.

Since self-described Democrats and Republicans both voted strongly along party lines in 2008, Obama's comfortable winning margin over McCain was largely a result of his 52 to 44 percent edge among independents, according to CNN's exit poll analysis. But in 2010, when Republicans made a big comeback in the midterm elections, CNN's exit polling of those voting nationally in House races showed that independents had swung sharply to the GOP, favoring the party by 56 to 37 percent over the Democrats.

Obama will again be counting on a strong turnout among African American voters, who according to exit polling favored him with 95 percent of their votes to 4 percent for McCain in 2008. Hispanics favored Obama over McCain by 66 to 32 percent, and the hard-line on immigration issues that many Hispanics perceived from Romney and most other Republicans virtually assures that the president will again have a strong advantage with this constituent group.

And the Obama campaign will be using its strong grasp on New Media communications to try to regenerate the level of enthusiasm he attracted from the nation's youngest voters in 2008. That year exit polls showed that Obama received 66 percent from voters eighteen to twenty-nine years of age, which was 12 percentage points better than what Democrat Kerry received among the same age cohort in 2004.

The Fights for Congress

While Obama still had to make up considerable ground he had lost in public support since his historic and relatively comfortable victory in 2008, it also was clear during spring 2012 that the Republicans had not maintained the momentum they had built in the run-up to the midterm elections two years ago.

That provided Democrats with reason to hope that they might be able to hold onto their majority in the Senate, something viewed as highly unlikely in the aftermath of the party's 2010 debacle. It also appears quite possible that they could at least cut into the Republican majority's 25-seat cushion in the House—and perhaps even reclaim a narrow majority, if an Obama surge in the fall campaign were to turn this into an unexpectedly strong Democratic year.

The terrible job approval ratings for Congress as a whole—ranging from 12 to 17 percent in three independent polls conducted in April—are not necessarily indicative of which party might have the advantage this November, because some of that is Democrats who blame all the problems on Republicans and vice versa. But other polling indicates that while both parties in Congress are unpopular, the public, to at least a slight degree or greater in some surveys, blames the Republicans more.

A McClatchy-Marist poll conducted March 20 through 22 showed that 34 percent of respondents approved of the Democrats' performance in Congress while 59 percent disapproved compared with 31 percent approval and 62 percent disapproval for Republicans. The gap was much wider in a *Washington Post*-ABC News poll taken a couple of weeks earlier, which pegged the Democrats at 34 percent approval and 60 percent disapproval, with 23 percent approval and 71 percent disapproval for the Republicans.

The Senate Campaign Landscape

This advantage in the polls is not big enough to guarantee the Democrats that they will be able to hold their Senate majority, which was trimmed from 59 to 53 seats in the tough 2010 elections.

The biggest obstacle that Democrats face is, ironically, the ripple effect of the very strong year they had in the 2006 midterm campaign, when the party won 6 Republican-held seats without losing any of their own. As a result, it is not a level playing field this year, with the seats of 23 incumbents who caucus with the Democrats (including 2 independents) up for election compared with 10 held by Republicans.

Open seats, meaning those occupied by incumbents who are not seeking reelection, are historically more difficult for the defending party to hold than those in which the incumbent is running, and Democrats face an imbalance there too, with 7 open seats to the Republicans' 3.

Yet a Republican majority in the upcoming 113rd Congress is not viewed as being as much of a given as it was in the wake of the GOP's big 2010 comeback.

Election prognosticators view the seats left open by retiring Democrats in two generally Republican-leaning states—Kent Conrad of North Dakota and Ben Nelson of Nebraska—to be the most vulnerable to takeover. Republicans are also staging strong bids to unseat Democratic incumbents Claire McCaskill of Missouri and Jon Tester of Montana, and capture open Democratic seats in Virginia, New Mexico, and Wisconsin. So if November brings another strong wave of Republican voting, it may be difficult for the Democrats to stave off serious losses.

If Obama gains an upper hand, however, he could not only help Democrats limit their losses but also to possibly offset them with victories over incumbents Scott P. Brown in Democratic-leaning Massachusetts and Dean Heller in politically competitive Nevada. And Democrats received a couple of unexpected opportunities to cut their losses with the surprise retirement announcement in February by the popular Maine Republican

Olympia J. Snowe, one of the last true moderates in the overwhelmingly conservative ranks of Senate Republicans, and the May primary defeat of six-term Republican senator Richard G. Lugar, an establishment conservative whose long history of bipartisan appeal turned into a negative for the riled Tea Party wing of the Republican Party.

Table 4 shows all the Senate races scheduled this year, the name of the incumbent, whether he or she is running this year, the result in the most recent election for the seat, and the predictions of this year's election outcomes, current as of June 2012, by two of the nation's leading prognosticators: Larry Sabato, a University of Virginia political scientist who publishes the Crystal Ball political website, and Charlie Cook, a veteran political journalist whose Cook Political Report is published by *National Journal* in Washington, D.C.

The following are short synopses of key races to watch.

Democratic Seats Most at Risk

Florida: The Democratic incumbent Bill Nelson, seeking a third Senate term, did not have flourishing job approval ratings, and he could be in trouble if Romney runs strongly in this conservative-leaning state. He nonetheless held double-digit leads in polls this spring over all candidates in the crowded August 14 Republican primary field that included Connie Mack, the four-term U.S. representative.

Hawaii: The decision by eighty-seven-year-old Daniel K. Akaka to retire after twenty-two years in the Senate creates a rare opening in Hawaii's tradition-bound Senate delegation that also includes nine-term incumbent Daniel K. Inouye. The state is a longtime Democratic stronghold, and Obama, who was born in Honolulu and received a record 72 percent of the vote in 2008, should again run strongly here. But the Democrats face a competitive August 11 primary between three-term 2nd District representative Mazie K. Hirono and her predecessor, Ed Case, who gave up his House seat for a 2006 Senate primary challenge to Akaka that failed. And Republicans have hopes for the former two-term governor Linda Lingle.

Missouri: Claire McCaskill's 2 percentage-point victory margin to unseat Republican incumbent Jim Talent in 2006 would have marked her as a GOP target even if 2012 were a stronger Democratic year. Missouri, a traditional swing state, has gone Republican for president in the past three elections, albeit by a razor-thin margin in 2008, so McCaskill can't expect a huge boost from Obama at the top of the ticket. But her efforts to project a relatively moderate image should keep her in the running, and Republicans have an August 7 primary between six-term U.S. representative Todd Akin, former state Treasurer Sarah Steelman, and businessman John Brunner, a campaign that could get fractious.

Montana: Jon Tester unseated three-term Republican incumbent Conrad Burns by just less than a 1 percentage-point margin in 2006. Because Montana generally has a

Missouri's Claire McCaskill, one of the Democrats' most endangered incumbents in this year's elections, at a meeting with constituents in Warrensburg, Mo., on April 9, 2012.

Republican lean, Tester faces a tough fight to win a second term, and his likely challenger, Denny Rehberg, is well-known statewide as the state's only U.S. House member for twelve years. But Tester, with his flat-top haircut and farming background, retains the down-home qualities that helped him get elected in the first place.

Nebraska: Ben Nelson's positioning as one of the nation's most prominent conservative-leaning Democrats enabled him to break the Republicans' strong grip in Nebraska. But after two terms as governor (1991–1999) and two in the Senate, Nelson is retiring, which appears to give the Republicans one of their best takeover opportunities this year. Still, a greater degree of uncertainty crept into the race in the May 15 primary, in which previously little-known state Senator Deb Fischer scored a stunning upset over state Attorney General Jon Bruning, the campaign's heavily favored front-runner. That could give an opportunity to Democrat Bob Kerrey, who was once popular as governor (1983–1987) and senator (1989–2001). Kerrey has the statewide political experience that Fischer lacks, but it's unclear how much of a welcome back he'll get after leaving politics and Nebraska to become a college president in New York City almost twelve years ago.

New Mexico: This seat would have been one of the Democrats' least worries had Jeff Bingaman—the winner of 71 percent of the vote in his 2006 reelection bid—sought a sixth term. But Bingaman is retiring, and New Mexico, though somewhat

TABLE 4
Senate Races 2012

State	Incumbent	Status	Most recent election (winner, %, victory margin)	Larry Sabato rating[a]	Charlie Cook rating[a]
Democratic seats (23)					
California	Dianne Feinstein	Seeking reelection	Feinstein 59%, +24	Safe Democratic	Solid Democratic
Connecticut	Joseph I. Lieberman[b]	Retiring	Lieberman 50%, +10	Likely Democratic	Likely Democratic
Delaware	Thomas R. Carper	Seeking reelection	Carper 70%, +41	Safe Democratic	Solid Democratic
Florida	Bill Nelson	Seeking reelection	Nelson 60%, +22	Toss up	Leans Democratic
Hawaii	Daniel K. Akaka	Retiring	Akaka 61%, +25	Leans Democratic	Toss up
Maryland	Benjamin L. Cardin	Seeking reelection	Cardin 54%, +10	Safe Democratic	Solid Democratic
Michigan	Debbie Stabenow	Seeking reelection	Stabenow 57%, +16	Likely Democratic	Leans Democratic
Minnesota	Amy Klobuchar	Seeking reelection	Klobuchar 58%, +20	Safe Democratic	Solid Democratic
Missouri	Claire McCaskill	Seeking reelection	McCaskill 50%, +2	Toss up	Toss up
Montana	Jon Tester	Seeking reelection	Tester 49%, +1	Toss up	Toss up
Nebraska	Ben Nelson	Retiring	Nelson 64%, +28%	Likely Republican	Likely Republican
New Jersey	Robert Menendez	Seeking reelection	Menendez 53%, +9	Likely Democratic	Likely Democratic
New Mexico	Jeff Bingaman	Retiring	Bingaman 71%, +42	Leans Democratic	Toss up
New York	Kirsten Gillibrand	Seeking reelection	Gillibrand 63%, +28 (2010)[c]	Safe Democratic	Solid Democratic
North Dakota	Kent Conrad	Retiring	Conrad 69%, +39	Leans Republican	Toss up
Ohio	Sherrod Brown	Seeking reelection	Brown 56%, +12	Leans Democratic	Leans Democratic
Pennsylvania	Bob Casey	Seeking reelection	Casey 59%, +17	Likely Democratic	Likely Democratic
Rhode Island	Sheldon Whitehouse	Seeking reelection	Whitehouse 53%, +6	Safe Democratic	Solid Democratic
Vermont	Bernard Sanders[b]	Seeking reelection	Sanders 65%, +33	Safe Independent	Solid Independent
Virginia	Jim Webb	Retiring	Webb 50%, +0.4	Toss up	Toss up

(Continued)

State	Incumbent	Status	Most recent election (winner, %, victory margin)	Larry Sabato rating[a]	Charlie Cook rating[a]
Washington	Maria Cantwell	Seeking reelection	Cantwell 57%, +17	Safe Democratic	Solid Democratic
West Virginia	Joe Manchin III	Seeking reelection	Manchin 53%, +10 (2010)[d]	Safe Democratic	Likely Democratic
Wisconsin	Herb Kohl	Retiring	Kohl 67%, +38	Toss up	Toss up
Republican seats (10)					
Arizona	Jon Kyl	Retiring	Kyl 53%, +10	Leans Republican	Likely Republican
Indiana	Richard G. Lugar	Defeated by Richard Mourdock in May 8 primary	Lugar 87%, +75	Leans Republican	Leans Republican
Maine	Olympia J. Snowe	Retiring	Snowe 74%, +54	Leans Independent[e]	Toss up
Massachusetts	Scott P. Brown	Seeking reelection	Brown 52%, +5 (2010)[f]	Toss up	Toss up
Mississippi	Roger Wicker	Seeking reelection	Wicker 64%, +29	Safe Republican	Solid Republican
Nevada	Dean Heller	Seeking reelection	John Ensign, R, 55%, +14[g]	Toss up	Toss up
Tennessee	Bob Corker	Seeking reelection	Corker 51%, +3	Safe Republican	Solid Republican
Texas	Kay Bailey Hutchison	Retiring	Hutchison 62%, +26	Safe Republican	Solid Republican
Utah	Orrin G. Hatch	June 26 primary	Hatch 63%, +32	Safe Republican	Solid Republican
Wyoming	John Barrasso	Seeking reelection	Barrasso 73%, +47 (2008)[h]	Safe Republican	Solid Republican

[a]Ratings, current as of June 7, 2012, are from the Crystal Ball website published by the University of Virginia political scientist Larry Sabato and *National Journal*'s Cook Political Report, headed by veteran journalist Charlie Cook.

[b]Lieberman and Sanders won in 2006 as independent candidates and served as Independents, but they caucused with the Senate Democrats.

[c]Gillibrand was appointed in 2009 to replace Democrat Hillary Rodham Clinton, the 2006 winner, who resigned to become President Obama's secretary of state. Gillibrand then won a November 2010 special election to fill the remainder of the unexpired term.

[d]Manchin won a November 2010 special election to fill out the remainder of the unexpired term of Democrat Robert C. Byrd, who won the 2006 election but died in June 2010. Manchin succeeded Democrat Carte Goodwin, who had been appointed to the vacancy on a temporary basis.

[e]Angus King, an independent who served as Maine governor from 1995 to 2003, is regarded as the front-running candidate for this open seat. He has not stated with which party he would caucus in the Senate but is widely seen as more likely to align with the Democrats.

[f]Brown won a January 2010 special election to fill out the remainder of the unexpired term of Democrat Edward M. Kennedy, who won the 2006 election but died in August 2009. Brown succeeded Democrat Paul G. Kirk Jr., who had been appointed to the vacancy on a temporary basis.

[g]Heller was appointed to fill out the remainder of Ensign's unexpired term after the incumbent resigned his seat in April 2011. The Nevada election this year is for a full six-year term.

[h]Barrasso was appointed in June 2007 to replace Republican Craig Thomas, who won the 2006 election but died in office. Barrasso then won a 2008 special election to fill the remainder of the unexpired term.

Democratic-leaning, can produce some very competitive elections. Two-term U.S. representative Martin Heinrich defeated state auditor Hector Balderas in the June 5 Democratic primary and will meet Republican Heather A. Wilson, who preceded Heinrich in the 1st Congressional District seat but lost a 2008 GOP Senate primary.

North Dakota: This state generally has such a strong Republican lean that Democratic candidates for president have carried it only five times and never since 1964. Yet for twenty-four years beginning in 1986, the state's two senators and at-large House member were all Democrats. The Republicans ended that anomaly in 2010 with John Hoeven's win for an open Senate seat and Rick Berg's upset of nine-term representative Earl Pomeroy. The GOP hopes that the retirement of four-term Democratic senator Kent Conrad will enable them to continue that roll, with Berg seeking to move from the House to the Senate after only two years. But the Democrats, who otherwise have a weak bench in North Dakota, produced a potentially competitive candidate in the former state attorney general Heidi Heitkamp, who lost to Hoeven for governor in 2000 but has received positive attention for fighting breast cancer during that campaign.

Virginia: The race for the seat left open by one-term Democrat Jim Webb is a classic battle of political titans, with former governor Tim Kaine running for the

Former Virginia governor Tim Kaine, running to defend the open Virginia Senate seat, addresses a campaign rally for President Obama in Richmond on May 5, 2012. To win, Kaine must rebuff a comeback attempt by Republican George Allen, who lost the seat to Democrat Jim Webb after one term in 2006. Webb decided to retire rather than seek a second term.

Democrats and George Allen—another former governor who held this Senate seat for a term before narrowly losing to Webb in 2006—seeking a comeback. Allen, an outspoken and sometimes acerbic conservative, had been regarded by a number of Republicans as a rising star on the national scene and possibly a 2008 presidential contender, but gaffes, most notably a barb he aimed at a Webb supporter during the 2006 contest that was widely portrayed as a racial slur, contributed greatly to his upset defeat. Kaine was popular as governor from 2006 to 2010, but to win this race, he may need another strong Virginia showing by Obama, who won the longtime Republican stronghold turned swing state by 7 percentage points in 2008.

Wisconsin: As with Bingaman in New Mexico, the decision by four-term incumbent Herb Kohl turned Wisconsin from a nearly certain Democratic hold into a major headache for the party. Wisconsin has swung more than even most swing states, giving Obama a 14-point victory margin in 2008 but just two years later electing Tea Party favorite Ron Johnson to the Senate over three-term Democrat Russ Feingold and electing conservative Scott Walker as governor. Walker's aggressive efforts to restrict collective bargaining for state workers spurred a backlash that produced a June 5 recall election, and the Democrats' Senate nominee, Tammy Baldwin, has a strong winning record in her House contests. But her mainly liberal views reflect her 2nd District, which includes the state capital of Madison and the University of Wisconsin, and the Republicans will be fielding a strong contender. The front-runner for the August 14 GOP primary was comeback-seeking Tommy G. Thompson, who was a popular governor from 1987 to 2001 before leaving to become U.S. secretary of Health and Human Services. But Thompson's long-shot bid for the 2008 Republican presidential nomination was brief and dismal, and he faced serious primary opposition from the state assembly speaker Jeff Fitzgerald and the former U.S. representative Mark Neumann.

Republican Seats Most at Risk

Indiana: Richard G. Lugar was widely regarded in the Washington establishment as one of the Senate's leading statesmen, an image that enabled him to win six terms, the last, in 2006, without a Democratic opponent. But in 2012, he was abruptly overtaken by the hot political tempers of the times. His proclivity for reaching across the partisan aisle, especially on the defense and foreign policy issues that became his specialties, increasingly irked conservative activists who aligned strongly with Tea Party candidate Richard Mourdock in his May 8 primary challenge. Mourdock's crushing win with 61 percent of the vote underscores that Republicans have a strong conservative base that gives him a serious chance of winning the November election in this generally Republican-leaning state. But his almost certain lack of the kind of bipartisan appeal Lugar showed throughout his career immediately turned this into a competitive race, and Democrats have a solid nominee in U.S. representative Joe Donnelly, who won

Indiana treasurer Richard Mourdock speaks to a victory rally in Indianapolis on May 8, 2012, after his stunning upset primary win over six-term Republican incumbent Richard G. Lugar.

three terms in the north-central 2nd District that is anything but a Democratic stronghold.

Maine: Maine shifted in recent decades from a longtime Republican stronghold to a place where Democratic presidential candidates have won five consecutive contests (including Obama's blowout by an 18-point margin in 2008). Olympia Snowe defied the trend to win three Senate terms by pursuing a much more centrist path than most of her Republican colleagues, and her decision to retire—which she attributed strongly to the deepened partisan divisiveness in Congress—handed Democrats one of their strongest opportunities. That is, if Angus King, a political independent who was the state's highly popular governor from 1995 to 2003, wins the November election. King quickly emerged as the front-runner, Democrats almost as quickly gave him their tacit endorsement, and his moderate profile has led to expectations that he would caucus with the Democrats if elected. Republicans say they will fight to hold this seat, citing the win by conservative Paul R. LePage for governor in 2010. But even in that strong Republican year, LePage received just 38 percent and won largely because the Democratic vote was split between the party's nominee and an independent candidate.

Massachusetts: Republican Scott P. Brown's stunning victory in the January 2010 special election for the seat long held by the liberal Democratic icon Edward M. Kennedy was an omen of how bad that election year was going to be for the Democrats. But Brown, running for a full term in the presidential election year of 2012, faces a tough fight to prove that victory was not a fluke. Obama, who carried the state by 26 points in 2008, is again expected to win easily, even though Republican challenger Romney was governor of Massachusetts from 2003 through 2006. Brown has broken with his conservative Republican Senate colleagues on some issues, which could bolster his contention that he is moderate enough to continue representing one of the nation's premier Democratic strongholds. Elizabeth Warren, a well-known consumer advocate who was the early favorite to win the September 6 Democratic primary, is something of a political lightning rod: She is regarded as a hero to many in the Democrats' liberal base, but Republicans, who brand her as a radical, in 2010 blocked her nomination by Obama to head the new federal Consumer Financial Protection Bureau.

Nevada: A gradual swing of Nevada from its longtime Republican leanings to a Democratic tilt appeared to blossom in 2008 when Obama defeated McCain by 12 points, in part because of the support he drew from the state's fast-growing Hispanic population. But Nevada, which had boomed over the previous decade, was among the states hit hardest by the economic downturn, and the voter anger that resulted forced Senate majority leader Harry Reid to fight for his political life in 2010 before securing a fifth term in a close race with Tea Party candidate Sharron Angle. The political pendulum appears to have swung back toward the middle, with Nevada looking very much in play for Obama, and incumbent Republican senator Dean Heller is still establishing himself statewide after he was picked out of the House seat in the northern 2nd District in April 2011 to fill the vacancy created when a personal scandal forced Republican incumbent John Ensign to resign from the Senate. The Democratic nominee, Shelley Berkley, has a strong electoral track record in her seven terms representing the 1st Congressional District but must expand strongly outside her Las Vegas base in order to win.

House: Ain't Mean a Thing if It Ain't Got That Swing

In the House it would be hard even under the best of circumstances for the Republicans to gain many more seats than they already have, if only because their 63-seat net gain two years ago was so outsized. The 242 seats that Republicans held as of June 2012 was their highest share in sixty-four years.

The Republican surge in 2010 proved especially timely, though, as party gains at the state level—governorships and legislative seats—put the party in strong position to benefit from congressional redistricting that took place after the December 2010 release of the latest national population census. An ambitiously partisan redistricting plan enacted by Republicans in North Carolina is viewed by pundits as likely to produce a gain of at least 2 and possibly as many as 4 seats, while Republican-drawn plans in states such as Pennsylvania, Virginia, Ohio, and Michigan appeared to shore up gains the party had made in 2010.

The Democrats, however, are expected to make redistricting-related gains in Illinois, one of the few states in which the party maintained full control of the remapping process after the 2010 elections, and the party looks like it could benefit with seat gains in California, a state where a newly established independent commission executed a sweeping overhaul of the congressional map.

Elizabeth Warren, a well-known consumer advocate who is seeking to challenge Republican senator Scott P. Brown in Massachusetts, chats on April 26, 2012, with a student at the Bricklayers and Allied Craftsman union apprenticeship program in Dorchester, Mass.

And given the highly volatile nature of U.S. politics over the past three election cycles, yet another major pendulum swing back to the Democrats cannot be completely ruled out. After Democrats gained 30 seats in 2006 and another 21 in 2008, and Republicans responded with a 63-seat gain in 2010, the 25-seat gain Democrats currently need to reclaim a bare majority does not seem like an impassable obstacle.

Five months out from election day, the rankings produced by major political pundits did not suggest a major wave of Democratic takeovers was rising. The ratings on Larry Sabato's Crystal Ball on June 7 showed Democrats either favored or were running competitive races to take over Republican seats in thirty-three districts, while Republicans faced similar odds in races for 28 Democratic seats.

But Democrats might take hope from the fact that there were late-breaking surges in both of the recent elections that resulted in a partisan takeover in the House: their own big year in 2006 and the Republicans' comeback in 2010.

Republicans Have Best Governor Race Opportunities

That 2010 Republican wave hit the state level too and produced a 6-seat gain that sent the GOP from a 26D-23R-1I disadvantage to a 29-20-1 advantage in the nation's governor seats. And the Democrats may need a very strong showing by Obama at the top of the ticket to avoid another deep setback this year.

There are only eleven contests this year, as most states schedule their races for governors for midterm or odd-numbered "off-year" elections (Table 5). But even more so than in the Senate campaigns, the Democrats have more at risk, defending 8 seats to the Republicans' 3 (as detailed in the accompanying chart). And while the GOP looks nearly certain to hold its seats in Indiana, North Dakota, and Utah, the Democrats appear to face tough fights for at least 4 of their seats in Montana, New Hampshire, North Carolina, and Washington.

Montana: Brian Schweitzer, a folksy and colorful rancher turned politician, won the governor's seat in 2004 and proved so popular he won reelection in 2008 by a 2–1 ratio. But Montana has a two-term limit, and Republicans are putting up a strong bid to reclaim the seat in a state that usually leans their way. Steve Bullock, the state attorney general, will defend the seat for the Democrats against Republican Rick Hill, a former two-term U.S. House member (1997–2001) who prevailed over a crowded field in the June 5 primary.

New Hampshire: New Hampshire and neighboring Vermont are the only states that have two-year terms for governor. Democrat John Lynch won his first election narrowly in 2004, then he quickly grew so popular that he won by a 42-point margin in 2006 and by 50 points in 2008. Even Lynch, though, was burdened by the Democratic downturn in 2010—his margin was trimmed back to 8 points—and he decided to retire rather than run again this year. Both parties have multicandidate fields for the September 11 primary.

North Carolina: Just four years ago, the presidential race produced a breakthrough in North Carolina, with Obama narrowly becoming the first Democrat to carry the state for president since 1976. The strong Democratic organizing effort there helped Bev Perdue, then the lieutenant governor, eke out a 3-point win over Republican Pat McCrory, a longtime mayor of Charlotte. But a backlash spurred a conservative resurgence in the state, and Perdue's job approval ratings declined, prompting her to opt out of a reelection bid this year. The Republicans nominated McCrory to take another crack at the governor's office, while Democratic primary voters on May 8 picked Lt. Gov. Walter Dalton.

Washington: The state anchoring the Pacific Northwest emerged in recent years as one of the nation's most consistently Democratic voting. The last Republican to win for president was Ronald Reagan in his 1984 landslide, Democrats hold both Senate seats, and the party has a seven-election winning streak for governor. But some of those governor's races have been nail-biters, no more so that the 2004 contest in which Christine Gregoire defeated Republican Dino Rossi by 133 votes, or less than one-hundredth of a percentage point. Gregoire won a more comfortable 6-point margin in a 2008 rematch with Rossi, but her decision to retire this year created

TABLE 5
Governor Races 2012

State	Incumbent	Status	Most recent election (winner, %, victory margin), all races in 2008 unless noted	Larry Sabato rating[a]	Charlie Cook rating[a]
Democratic seats					
Delaware	Jack Markell	Seeking reelection	Markell 68%, +36	Safe Democratic	Solid Democratic
Missouri	Jay Nixon	Seeking reelection	Nixon 58%, +19	Likely Democratic	Leans Democratic
Montana	Brian Schweitzer	Retiring (term limit)	Schweitzer 65%, +32	Leans Republican	Toss up
New Hampshire	John Lynch	Retiring	Lynch 53%, +8 (2010)	Toss up	Toss up
North Carolina	Beverly Perdue	Retiring	Perdue 50%, +3	Leans Republican	Leans Republican
Vermont	Peter Shumlin	Seeking reelection	Shumlin 50%, +2 (2010)	Safe Democratic	Solid Democratic
Washington	Christine Gregoire	Retiring	Gregoire 53%, +6	Toss up	Toss up
West Virginia	Earl Ray Tomblin	Seeking reelection	Tomblin 49%, +2 (2011)[b]	Leans Democratic	Leans Democratic
Republican seats					
Indiana	Mitch Daniels	Retiring (term limit)	Daniels 58%, +18	Likely Republican	Likely Republican
North Dakota	Jack Dalrymple	Running for full term	John Hoeven, R, 74%, +50[c]	Safe Republican	Solid Republican
Utah	Gary R. Herbert	Seeking re-election	Herbert 64%, +32% (2010)[d]	Safe Republican	Solid Republican

[a]Ratings, current as of May 6, 2012, are from the Crystal Ball website published by the University of Virginia political scientist Larry Sabato and *National Journal*'s Cook Political Report, headed by the veteran journalist Charlie Cook.

[b]Tomblin filled the vacancy created in November 2010 when Democratic predecessor Joe Manchin won a special election to fill the unexpired term of the late Democratic senator Robert C. Byrd. Tomblin then won an October 2011 special election to retain the seat.

[c]Hoeven won a third term as governor in 2008, but resigned after winning the U.S. Senate election in 2010. Dalrymple, then lieutenant governor, moved up to succeed him.

[d]Herbert moved up from lieutenant governor in August 2009 to succeed Republican Jon Huntsman Jr., who had been confirmed as U.S. ambassador to China. State law required a special election in November 2010 to fill out the remainder of Huntsman's unexpired term, which Herbert won. This year's election is for a full four-year term.

an open-seat race that is expected to be highly competitive. Both parties settled early on their nominees with Democrats choosing eight-term U.S. representative Jay Inslee and Republicans tapping state attorney general Rob McKenna for a strong takeover bid.

⑤SAGE research**methods**

The essential online tool for researchers from the world's leading methods publisher

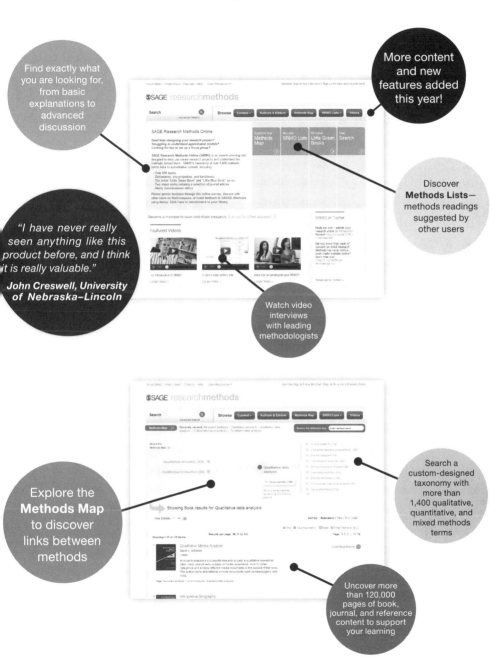

Find exactly what you are looking for, from basic explanations to advanced discussion

More content and new features added this year!

"I have never really seen anything like this product before, and I think it is really valuable."
John Creswell, University of Nebraska–Lincoln

Discover **Methods Lists**— methods readings suggested by other users

Watch video interviews with leading methodologists

Explore the **Methods Map** to discover links between methods

Search a custom-designed taxonomy with more than 1,400 qualitative, quantitative, and mixed methods terms

Uncover more than 120,000 pages of book, journal, and reference content to support your learning

Find out more at
www.sageresearchmethods.com